I0455219

July 2013

SECURITIES AND EXCHANGE COMMISSION

Improving Personnel Management Is Critical for Agency's Effectiveness

GAO-13-621

GAO Highlights

Highlights of GAO-13-621, a report to congressional committees

SECURITIES AND EXCHANGE COMMISSION
Improving Personnel Management Is Critical for Agency's Effectiveness

Why GAO Did This Study

Personnel management is important to the mission of federal agencies. Several high-profile enforcement failures have raised concerns about SEC's personnel management. Section 962 of the Dodd-Frank Wall Street Reform and Consumer Protection Act mandates GAO to report on SEC's personnel management. This report examines (1) SEC's organizational culture and (2) its personnel management challenges and efforts to address these challenges.

GAO assessed SEC's personnel management systems against OPM guidance and other criteria related to workforce planning and performance management (which includes appraisals and feedback); reviewed relevant reports; surveyed SEC employees and senior management (with 78 and 74 percent response rates, respectively) to gather their views on SEC's organizational culture and personnel management practices; and spoke with former employees, the SEC Inspector General, representatives of the employees' union, financial industry associations, consulting firms, and academics.

What GAO Recommends

GAO makes seven recommendations to improve SEC's personnel management, including developing comprehensive workforce plans, implementing mechanisms to monitor how supervisors use the performance management system, conducting periodic validations of the system, exploring collaboration practices of leading organizations, and regularly assessing these efforts. SEC agreed with GAO's recommendations.

View GAO-13-621. For more information, contact A. Nicole Clowers at (202) 512-8678 or clowersa@gao.gov.

What GAO Found

Based on analysis of views from Securities and Exchange Commission (SEC) employees and previous studies from GAO, SEC, and third parties, GAO determined that SEC's organizational culture is not constructive and could hinder its ability to effectively fulfill its mission. Organizations with constructive cultures are more effective and employees also exhibit a stronger commitment to mission focus. In describing SEC's culture, many current and former SEC employees cited low morale, distrust of management, and the compartmentalized, hierarchical, and risk-averse nature of the organization. According to an Office of Personnel Management (OPM) survey of federal employees, SEC currently ranks 19th of 22 similarly sized federal agencies based on employee satisfaction and commitment. GAO's past work on managing for results indicates that an effective personnel management system will be critical for transforming SEC's organizational culture.

SEC has not consistently or fully implemented effective personnel management. SEC has taken some steps, but most of its efforts were in the early stages and could be enhanced. GAO identified four key areas where continued improvement is needed:

- *Workforce planning.* SEC has not yet developed a comprehensive workforce plan, including how it identifies its future leaders. Although SEC has taken some steps, such as identifying competency gaps and conducting leadership training, these efforts do not reflect all elements of effective workforce planning outlined in OPM guidance. OPM guidance calls on agencies to develop and implement plans to identify workforce needs and develop future leaders. Without fully implementing such practices, SEC will not be able to make well-informed decisions on how to best meet current and future agency needs.

- *Performance management.* SEC's implementation of its performance management system could be improved. SEC staff expressed many concerns about the system, such as an unclear link between their performance and ratings. SEC provided training to supervisors on how to use the system and obtained staff input on aspects of the system. However, SEC has not fully validated the system with its staff. Also, SEC does not have mechanisms in place to monitor supervisors' use of the system. By not validating all aspects of the system and establishing mechanisms to hold supervisors accountable for appropriately using it, SEC is missing opportunities to enhance the credibility and effectiveness of its performance management system.

- *Communication and collaboration.* SEC has made efforts to improve communication and collaboration (such as creating new subunits to facilitate joint work), but has not yet fully addressed barriers. Moreover, these efforts have not yet addressed all of the problems that the Inspector General found contributed to past enforcement failures. GAO has reported on leading practices that SEC could explore, including sustained management attention. Improving communication and collaboration within SEC is critical to its effectiveness.

- *Personnel management assessment.* SEC has not implemented an accountability system to monitor and evaluate its personnel management. According to OPM guidance, such a system helps agencies assess whether personnel policies are effective. SEC officials explained that efforts were under way to develop a system. Until such an accountability system is implemented, it will be difficult for SEC to make necessary improvements and help ensure that its personnel management policies and programs align with its mission.

_____ **United States Government Accountability Office**

Contents

Abbreviations

COO	Office of the Chief Operating Officer
DERA	Division of Economic and Risk Analysis
FAA	Federal Aviation Administration
HCAAF	Human Capital Assessment and Accountability Framework
IG	Inspector General
NEP	National Examination Program
OCIE	Office of Compliance Inspections and Examinations
OHR	Office of Human Resources
OPM	Office of Personnel Management
SEC	Securities and Exchange Commission

July 18, 2013

The Honorable Tim Johnson
Chairman
The Honorable Michael Crapo
Ranking Member
Committee on Banking, Housing, and Urban Affairs
United States Senate

The Honorable Jeb Hensarling
Chairman
The Honorable Maxine Waters
Ranking Member
Committee on Financial Services
House of Representatives

The Securities and Exchange Commission's (SEC) mission is to protect investors; maintain fair, orderly, and efficient securities markets; and facilitate capital formation. To carry out its mission, SEC requires public companies to disclose meaningful financial and other information to the public, examines firms it regulates, and investigates potential securities law violations. Over the past decade, the markets, products, and participants that SEC oversees and regulates—including investment advisers, mutual and exchange-traded funds, and broker-dealers—have grown in size and complexity. Trading volume in the equity markets has more than doubled, as have assets under management by investment advisers.

As the markets grew in size and complexity over the past two decades, investors experienced large losses during the 2007-2009 financial crisis and through a few high-profile fraud cases, such as the failure of Bernard L. Madoff Investment Securities LLC. The financial crisis highlighted the interconnectedness and complexity of the growing financial markets as securitized assets amplified losses across multiple markets. The crisis also highlighted gaps and weaknesses in the supervision and regulation of financial markets. To address such concerns, Congress enacted the Dodd-Frank Wall Street Reform and Consumer Protection Act (the Dodd-Frank Act).[1] Among other things, the act expands SEC's regulatory

---

[1] Pub. L. No. 111-203, 124 Stat. 1376 (2010).

responsibilities, including increased oversight of hedge funds and derivatives. However, members of Congress and other stakeholders have questioned SEC's ability to effectively protect investors in light of the growing complexity of the markets and past enforcement failures.

Effectively carrying out existing and new regulatory responsibilities requires that SEC attract and retain a high-quality workforce. However, we and others previously reported on the personnel management challenges SEC has faced in building and retaining such a workforce.[2] These challenges included a lack of emphasis on personnel management and weaknesses in linking pay and performance. SEC is not unique in facing personnel management challenges. In 2001, we added strategic human capital management to our list of high-risk areas because of the long-standing lack of leadership on personnel matters across the government.[3]

Section 962 of the Dodd-Frank Act mandates us to examine SEC's personnel management, including the competence of professional staff, the effectiveness of supervisors, and issues related to employee performance assessments, promotion, and intra-agency communication.[4]

---

[2]See GAO, *Securities and Exchange Commission: Human Capital Challenges Require Management Attention*, GAO-01-947 (Washington, D.C.: Sept. 17, 2001); *Securities and Exchange Commission: Human Capital Survey*, GAO-05-118R (Washington, D.C.: Nov. 10, 2004); *Securities and Exchange Commission: Some Progress Made on Strategic Human Capital Management*, GAO-06-86 (Washington, D.C.: Jan. 10, 2006); *Financial Regulators: Agencies Have Implemented Key Performance Management Practices, but Opportunities for Improvement Exist*, GAO-07-678 (Washington, D.C.: Jun. 18, 2007); and *Securities and Exchange Commission: Greater Attention Needed to Enhance Communication and Utilization of Resources in the Division of Enforcement*, GAO-09-358 (Washington, D.C.: Mar. 31, 2009). Also see SEC, Office of Inspector General, *Report on Enforcement Performance Management*, OIG-423 (Washington, D.C.: Feb. 8, 2007); *Investigation of Failure of the SEC to Uncover Bernard Madoff's Ponzi Scheme*, public version, OIG-509 (Washington, D.C.: Aug. 31, 2009); *Program Improvements Needed within the SEC's Division of Enforcement*, OIG-467 (Washington, D.C.: Sept. 29, 2009); *Investigation of the SEC's Response to Concerns Regarding Robert Allen Stanford's Alleged Ponzi Scheme*, public version,OIG-526 (Washington, D.C.: Mar. 31, 2010); and *OCIE Regional Offices' Referrals to Enforcement,* public version, OIG-493 (Washington, D.C.: Mar. 30, 2011). See Boston Consulting Group, *U.S. Securities and Exchange Commission: Organizational Study and Reform* (Washington, D.C.: Mar. 2011); and Robert Tobias, *Evaluation of the U.S. Securities and Exchange Commission's Evidence Based Performance Management System* (Washington, D.C.: June 1, 2012).

[3]For our most recent high-risk report, see GAO, *High-Risk Series: An Update*, GAO-13-283 (Washington, D.C.: Feb. 2013).

[4]Pub. L. No. 111-203, § 962, 124 Stat. 1376, 1908-09 (2010).

This report examines (1) what is known about SEC's organizational culture and (2) SEC's personnel management challenges and its efforts to address these challenges.[5]

To document SEC's organizational culture and personnel management challenges, we reviewed management consultant reports, GAO reports, and SEC reports and testimonies. We also interviewed former SEC officials, the SEC Inspector General (IG), SEC union representatives and members, management consultants, representatives from industry trade groups, and academics with knowledge of SEC personnel management issues. We examined SEC's performance management policies, procedures, and activities by reviewing agency documents related to workforce and succession planning (such as recruitment and training practices), performance appraisals, supervision, promotion processes, and communication within and among divisions. We assessed the policies, procedures, and activities against applicable federal regulations, the Office of Personnel Management's (OPM) Human Capital Assessment and Accountability Framework (HCAAF), key human capital practices and GAO standards for internal control, and SEC's strategic plan.[6]

We also conducted semistructured one-on-one interviews, focus groups, and two web-based surveys to gather employee views on SEC's organizational culture and the agency's personnel management practices,

---

[5]Organizational culture is the underlying assumptions, beliefs, values, attitudes, and expectations shared by an organization's members that affect their behavior and the behavior of the organization as a whole.

[6]Human Resources Management in Agencies, HCAAF and HCAAF Systems, Standards, and Metrics, 73 Fed. Reg. 23012, 23027 (Apr. 28, 2008) (codified at 5 C.F.R. § 250.202 (2012)); GAO, *Organizational Transformation: Implementing Chief Operating Officer/Chief Management Officer Positions in Federal Agencies*, GAO-08-34 (Washington, D.C.: Nov. 1, 2007); *Human Capital: Key Principles for Effective Workforce Planning*, GAO-04-39 (Washington, D.C.: Dec. 11, 2003); *Results-Oriented Cultures: Modern Performance Management Systems Are Needed to Effectively Support Pay for Performance*, GAO-03-612T (Washington, D.C.: Apr. 1, 2003); *Human Capital: DOD Needs to Improve Implementation of and Address Employee Concerns about its National Security Personnel System*, GAO-08-773 (Washington, D.C.: Sept. 10, 2008); *Results-Oriented Government: Practices That Can Help Enhance and Sustain Collaboration among Federal Agencies*, GAO-06-15 (Washington, D.C.: Oct. 21, 2005); *Managing Key Results: Key Considerations for Implementing Interagency Collaborative Mechanisms*, GAO-12-1022 (Washington, D.C.: Sept. 27, 2012); and *Standards for Internal Control in the Federal Government*, AIMD-00-21.3.1 (Washington, D.C.: Nov. 1999).

including areas where SEC has been doing well and areas in which there are challenges. The scope of these efforts included employees in the five divisions and one office (hereinafter, divisions) in SEC primarily responsible for implementing the agency's mission—Divisions of Corporation Finance; Enforcement; Investment Management; Economic and Risk Analysis; Trading and Markets; and the Office of Compliance Inspections and Examinations (OCIE).[7] In these divisions, we focused on employees in four occupational categories—accountants, attorneys, examiners, and financial analysts—that account for the majority of SEC employees. We held one-on-one interviews with 129 nonsupervisory staff, supervisors, and senior officers at SEC headquarters and regional offices from July to September 2012.[8] All employees in the relevant divisions and occupational categories were invited to participate in the interviews. We held 22 focus groups at headquarters and four regional offices with nonsupervisory staff and supervisors in the divisions and occupational categories within our scope. We selected the regional offices based on factors including enforcement activity, geographic location, and staff size, and randomly selected staff and supervisors from the relevant divisions for our focus groups. We also implemented two web-based surveys of all 2,439 employees (nonsupervisory staff and supervisory) and 86 senior officers in these divisions that fall within the four occupation groups.[9] The survey response rates were 78 and 74 percent, respectively. We do not make any attempt to extrapolate the findings to the 22 percent of eligible staff who chose not to complete our survey. We reviewed OPM's 2012 Federal Employee Viewpoint Survey Results to obtain additional perspectives from SEC staff on the agency's personnel management-

[7]On June 6, 2013, SEC renamed the Division of Risk, Strategy, and Financial Innovation to the Division of Economic and Risk Analysis (DERA).

[8]For the purposes of our surveys, (1) nonsupervisory staff are employees in SEC's pay plan grades SK 12-16 for the Division of Enforcement, and SK 12, 13, 14, and 16 for the remaining four divisions and OCIE; (2) supervisors are employees in SEC's pay plan grades SK 17 for the Division of Enforcement, and SK 15 and 17 for the other divisions and OCIE; and (3) senior officers are employees in SEC's pay plan grades SO 1-3. See the background section of this report for more information on the organizational structure of SEC.

[9]According to SEC data, this figure captures the number of staff who were employed as of September 30, 2012.

GAO-13-621 SEC Personnel Management

related issues.[10] Appendix I includes more information on our scope and methodology.

We conducted this performance audit from March 2012 to July 2013 in accordance with generally accepted government auditing standards. Those standards require that we plan and perform the audit to obtain sufficient and appropriate evidence to provide a reasonable basis for our findings and conclusions based on our audit objectives. We believe that the evidence obtained provides a reasonable basis for our findings and conclusions based on our audit objectives.

Background

SEC is composed of a five-member Commission that oversees SEC operations and provides final approval over staff interpretation of federal securities laws, proposals for new or amended rules to govern securities markets, and enforcement activities. The Commission, which is headed by the SEC chairman, oversees 5 divisions and 23 offices, including 11 regional offices. Figure 1 further depicts SEC's organizational structure.

---

[10]OPM's Federal Employee Viewpoint Survey is a tool that measures employees' perceptions of whether, and to what extent, conditions characterizing successful organizations are present in their agencies. Survey results provide valuable insight into the challenges agency leaders face in ensuring the government has an effective civilian workforce and how well they are responding. The 2012 Federal Employee Viewpoint Survey included employees from 82 agencies (constituting 97 percent of executive branch agencies).

Figure 1: Organizational Structure of SEC, as of September, 2012

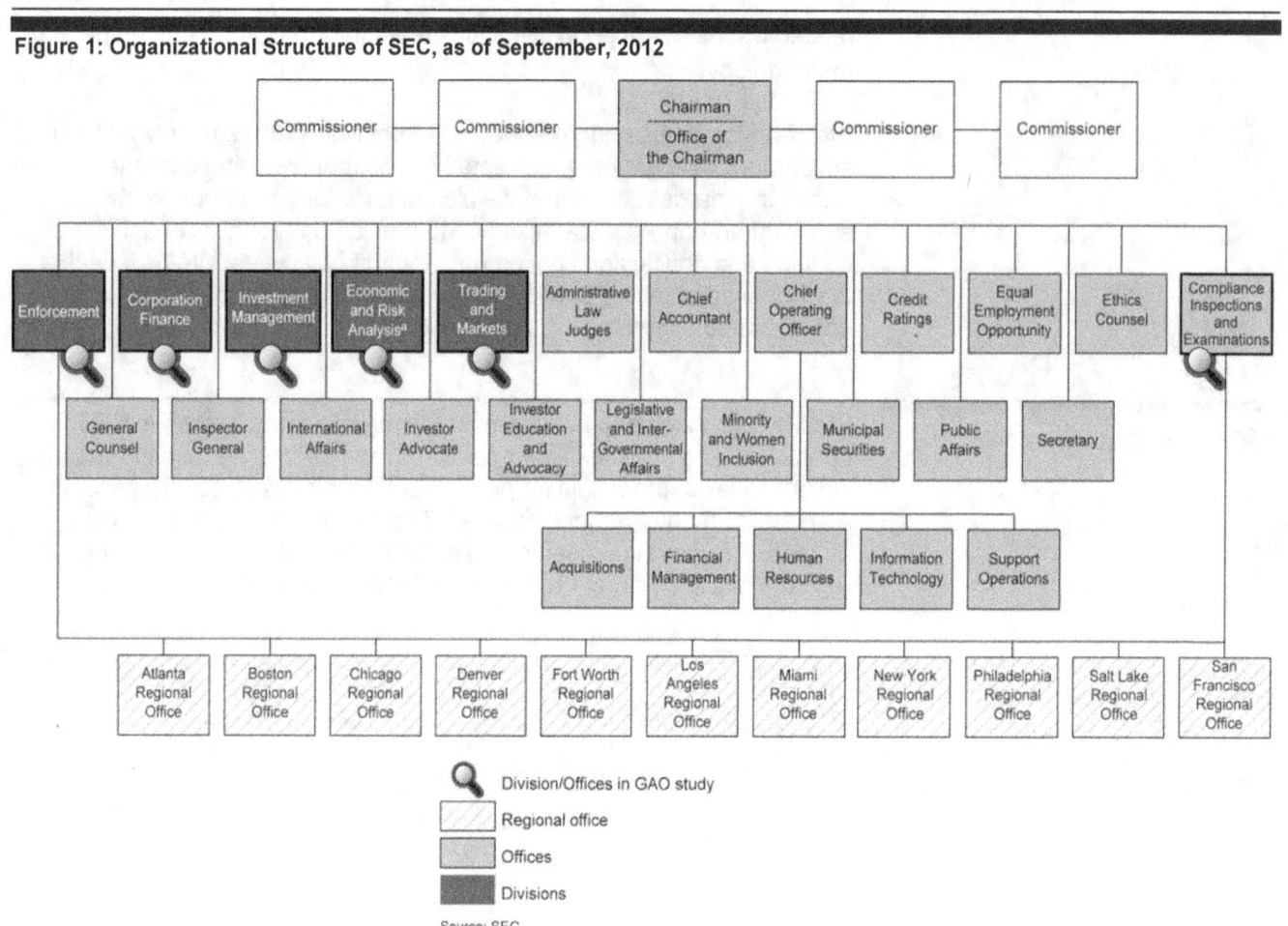

Source: SEC.

[a]On June 6, 2013, SEC renamed the Division of Risk, Strategy, and Financial Innovation to the Division of Economic and Risk Analysis.

SEC's divisions are organized by functional responsibility. For example, SEC's responsibilities for reviewing corporate disclosures are housed within the Division of Corporation Finance. Table 1 summarizes the roles and responsibilities of the six divisions that primarily implement SEC's mission. These divisions are supported by other offices, such as the Office of Financial Management and the Office of Human Resources (OHR). In particular, OHR provides overall responsibility for the strategic management of SEC's personnel management and assesses compliance with federal regulations for areas such as recruitment, retention, leadership and staff development, and performance management. OHR reports to SEC's Office of the Chief Operating Officer (COO), which in turn reports to the Commission.

Table 1: Roles and Responsibilities of Selected SEC Divisions, as of April 2013

Division	Roles and responsibilities
Division of Corporation Finance	Reviews corporate disclosures, assists companies in interpreting SEC's rules, and recommends new rules for adoption.
Division of Enforcement	Investigates possible violations of securities laws, recommends Commission action when appropriate, either in a federal court or before an administrative law judge, and negotiates settlements.
Division of Investment Management	Regulates investment companies (such as mutual, closed-end, and exchange-traded funds), some insurance products, and federally registered investment advisers.
Division of Economic and Risk Analysis[a]	Serves as SEC's "think tank" on economic issues. Associated with the entire range of SEC activities, including policymaking, rule making, enforcement, and examination. The division also assists in SEC's efforts to identify, analyze, and respond to risks and trends, including those associated with new financial products and strategies.
Division of Trading and Markets	Establishes and maintains standards for fair, orderly, and efficient markets. The division regulates major securities market participants, including the securities exchanges, broker-dealers, self-regulatory organizations, and transfer agents (parties that maintain records of stock and bond owners).
Office of Compliance Inspections and Examinations	Administers examination and inspection program of the registered entities, including broker-dealers, transfer agents, investment advisers, investment companies, national securities exchanges, clearing agencies, self-regulatory organizations, and the Public Company Accounting Oversight Board.

Source: SEC.

[a]On June 6, 2013, SEC renamed the Division of Risk, Strategy, and Financial Innovation to the Division of Economic and Risk Analysis.

To carry out its mission, SEC employs staff with a range of skills and backgrounds, such as attorneys, accountants, and economists. As of September 30, 2012, SEC employed 3,829 staff. Of these staff, approximately 43 percent were attorneys, 26 percent were accountants or financial analysts, and 4 percent were examiners. The remaining 27 percent were other professional, technical, administrative, and clerical staff. To help SEC attract and retain qualified employees, Congress enacted the Investor and Capital Markets Fee Relief Act (Pay Parity Act) in 2002 that allowed SEC to implement a new compensation system with unique pay scales comparable to those of other federal financial regulators.[11] SEC staff are represented by the National Treasury Employees Union (hereafter, the SEC employees' union).

SEC's Performance Management System

SEC's performance management system, also known as the Evidence-Based Performance Management System, includes individual development plans for all employees, a performance appraisal rating system, a feedback process, and a process for supervisors to deal with poor performance. The current performance appraisal system has criteria by which all SEC employees are rated in relation to work objectives and competency-based performance standards, such as critical thinking and teamwork. Staff are rated on the objectives and standards on a scale of 1-5.[12] SEC calculates an overall rating for each employee by averaging their ratings for the objectives and standards.[13] As designed, employees' ratings eventually would be used to calculate the employee's pay-for-performance. SEC developed this system in 2010 and continues to negotiate aspects of the design and implementation of its current performance management system with the SEC employees' union.[14] For example, to date SEC has not instituted the pay-for-performance aspect of the system for nonsupervisory, bargaining unit staff because of ongoing negotiations.

---

[11]Pub. L. No. 107-123, § 8, 115 Stat. 2390, 2397-99 (2002).

[12]Under SEC's system, a rating of 5 is defined as greatly exceeds expectations, 4 exceeds expectations, 3 meets expectations, 2 needs improvement, and 1 is unacceptable.

[13]There are slight differences in how ratings are calculated for employees covered by the bargaining and those not covered by the unit. For bargaining unit employees, scores for objectives have more weight than the scores for standards when the overall average scores are calculated. For nonbargaining unit employees, the objectives and standards scores are weighed equally when calculating the overall rating.

[14]On October 19, 2006, the Federal Services Impasse Panel ruled on Case No. 06 FSIP 54, In the Matter of SEC and the National Treasury Employees Union (the SEC employees' union). Several provisions in the panel decision related to SEC's performance management system, including a redesign of the system to include five levels of ratings. In response to the panel decision, SEC developed and implemented the Evidence-Based Performance Management System.

OPM's Human Capital Assessment and Accountability Framework

OPM advocates the use of HCAAF, which is a set of tools and strategies available to federal agencies that assist officials in achieving results in personnel management programs.[15] HCAAF guides the assessment of agency efforts, while allowing enough flexibility for agencies to tailor these efforts to their missions, plans, and budgets. The framework uses five standards for success, lists key questions to consider, and suggests performance indicators for measuring progress and results. The five standards for success are as follows:

- *Strategic alignment.* Agency strategies for human capital management are aligned with mission, goals, and organizational objectives and are integrated into its strategic plan and performance budget.
- *Leadership and knowledge management.* Agency leaders and managers effectively manage people, ensure continuity of leadership, sustain a learning environment that drives continuous improvement in performance, and provide a means to share critical knowledge across the organization.
- *Results-oriented performance culture.* The agency has a diverse, results-oriented, high-performing workforce and a performance management system that effectively differentiates between high and low levels of performance and links individual/team/unit performance to organizational goals and desired results.
- *Talent management.* The agency has closed gaps or deficiencies in skills, knowledge, and competencies for mission-critical occupations, and made meaningful progress toward closing such gaps or deficiencies in all occupations used in the agency.
- *Accountability.* A data-driven, results-oriented planning and accountability system guides the agency's decisions on human capital management.

OPM has been providing some updates to the HCAAF model to federal agencies; however, OPM officials with whom we spoke stated that agencies would continue operating under the current HCAAF model until the end of fiscal year 2013 because the updated version has not been fully implemented. They noted that the updates to HCAAF reinforce existing content and streamline the systems to make HCAAF more

---

[15]Human Resources Management in Agencies, HCAAF and HCAAF Systems, Standards, and Metrics, 73 Fed. Reg. 23012, 23027 (Apr. 28, 2008) (codified at 5 C.F.R. § 250.202 (2012)).

practical to use. The updated version of HCAAF, called the Human Capital Framework, reduces the number of systems from five to four (strategic alignment, talent management, performance culture, and evaluation).

SEC's Organizational Culture Hinders Agency's Ability to Effectively Fulfill Its Mission

Based on our analysis of the views of many SEC employees, our previously issued reports on SEC, and recent studies from SEC and third parties, we have determined that the agency's organizational culture is not constructive and could hinder its ability to effectively fulfill its mission. Organizations with more constructive cultures generally perform better and are more effective. Within constructive cultures, employees also exhibit a stronger commitment to mission focus, accountability, coordination, and adaptability.[16] In describing the agency's culture, many current and four former SEC employees talked about low levels of employee morale, employees' distrust of management, and the compartmentalized, hierarchical, and risk-averse nature of the organization. These views are consistent with our past work as well as the work of others.

SEC's culture reflects low employee morale. More than half of nonsupervisory staff and about 43 percent of supervisory staff disagreed that employee morale is generally high most of the time. About a quarter of senior officers had the same view (see table 2). We also found that 44.7 percent of nonsupervisory staff and 30 percent of supervisors did not agree that management has taken steps to improve employee morale.

---

[16]In a previous report, we focused on determining whether the Federal Aviation Administration's (FAA) culture affected its acquisitions. For the analysis, we drew extensively on studies by FAA and other organizations, surveyed FAA employees, and reviewed studies on organizational change and culture in the public and private sectors. In describing criteria for organizational culture, we noted that research has shown that in organizations with a more constructive culture, employees exhibit a stronger commitment to (1) mission focus (pursuing goals that define the best course of action for an organization); (2) accountability (empowering employees and holding them responsible for their decisions and actions); (3) coordination (involving other employees in decisions affecting them, resolving differences collaboratively, and cooperating across organizational lines); and (4) adaptability (accepting new approaches and responding positively to demands and opportunities posed from within and outside of the organization). We found FAA's acquisitions were impaired because employees acted in ways that did not reflect a strong commitment to mission focus, accountability, coordination, and adaptability. See GAO, *Aviation Acquisition: A Comprehensive Strategy Is Needed for Cultural Change at FAA,* GAO/RCED-96-159 (Washington, D.C.: Aug. 22, 1996).

Table 2: Survey Responses from SEC Employees about Morale, as of January-March 2013

Survey statement: *Employee morale is generally high most of the time.*

Response category	Nonsupervisory staff	Supervisory staff	Senior officers
Strongly agree/somewhat agree	29.8%	38.2%	54.7%
Neither agree or disagree	14.5	18.2	20.3
Strongly disagree/somewhat disagree	54.1	42.6	25.0
Do not know	1.2	0.8	0.0
No response checked	0.4	0.3	0.0
Total	**100**	**100**	**100**
(number of respondents)	**(1,462)**	**(390)**	**(64)**

Source: GAO.

Note: Percentages may not always add to 100 due to rounding.

According to a number of staff who provided written survey comments, morale is low for various reasons, ranging from lack of effective leadership and communication to dissatisfaction with the performance management system and opportunities for promotion. Furthermore, many staff who participated in our one-on-one interviews commented that the implementation of the five-point performance rating scale resulted in arbitrary ratings and that they perceived favoritism in promotions. Many other staff commented that staff morale was low. These sentiments were similar to our past findings. For example, we reported in 2001 that SEC had not created an organizational culture that ensured ongoing attention to personnel management issues and that SEC staff did not think the agency sufficiently valued and motivated staff.[17] Our findings in this report are also consistent with the Partnership for Public Service's analysis of OPM's 2012 Employee Viewpoint Survey.[18] The analysis found that SEC's overall index score—which measures staff's general satisfaction

---

[17]GAO-01-947.

[18]First issued in 2003, the Partnership for Public Service uses data from OPM's Federal Employee Viewpoint Survey to rank agencies and their subcomponents according to a Best Places to Work index score. The 2012 rankings draw on responses from nearly 700,000 civil servants to produce a detailed view of employee satisfaction and commitment across 362 federal agencies and subcomponents. Agencies and subcomponents not only are measured on overall employee satisfaction, but are scored in 10 workplace categories, such as effective leadership, employee skills/mission match, pay, teamwork, and work/life balance.

and commitment—declined from 73.1 in 2007 to 56 in 2012.[19] Compared with other midsize agencies, SEC ranked 19 of 22 in overall satisfaction and commitment. The decrease in morale among staff may negatively affect their productivity and commitment to the agency's mission.

SEC's culture reflects an atmosphere of distrust. When asked whether there is an atmosphere of trust at SEC, many staff disagreed. As shown in table 3, 40 percent of nonsupervisory staff and about 30 percent of supervisory staff thought there was a lack of trust. About 17 percent of senior officers voiced this viewpoint.

Table 3: Survey Responses from SEC Employees about Trust, as of January-March 2013

Survey statement: *There is an atmosphere of trust in my office/office.*

Response category	Nonsupervisory staff	Supervisory staff	Senior officers
Strongly agree/somewhat agree	45.1%	59.0%	73.4%
Neither agree or disagree	13.4	10.5	7.8
Strongly disagree/somewhat disagree	40.0	30.3	17.2
Do not know	1.1	0.3	1.6
No response checked	0.4	0	0
Total	**100**	**100**	**100**
(number of respondents)	**(1,462)**	**(390)**	**(64)**

Source: GAO.

Note: Percentages may not always add to 100 due to rounding.

Survey respondents offered explanations for the lack of trust. From their written comments on SEC's organizational culture, lack of trust was among the more frequently mentioned topics. For example, one survey respondent indicated that the atmosphere of distrust was due to a lack of direct communication with and knowledge sharing from managers. Based on comments from several respondents, the adverse working relationship between the union and management may have contributed to the level of distrust between staff and upper management by constantly assuming the worst in senior managers' initiatives and other actions. The lack of trust

---

[19]According to the Partnership for Public Service analysis, the government-wide satisfaction and commitment score in 2012 has dropped to the lowest point since rankings were first published in 2003. The declining job satisfaction levels across the federal government come during turbulent times, with employees feeling the effects of a 2- and 1/2 year pay freeze, hiring slowdowns, and budget constraints.

may undermine the working relationships between management and staff.

SEC's culture is compartmentalized. Many current and three former staff described SEC's culture as "siloed"—that is, work is compartmentalized in each division and little communication, collaboration, or movement occurs between the divisions. Despite recent SEC efforts to improve intra-agency communication that we discuss later in this report, issues remain. According to our survey, at least one-third of nonsupervisory staff and supervisors said that in the past 12 months, they had not contacted staff in other divisions (except for Enforcement) in the home office for work-related issues, such as coordinating activities or asking for expert advice.[20] Further, about 21 percent of nonsupervisory staff said that communication between other divisions on work-related matters is not encouraged.[21] Others have identified similar issues. For example, a 2009 SEC IG report found that the Division of Enforcement did not always seek assistance from other offices and divisions as needed during its investigation of the Madoff Ponzi scheme; consequently Enforcement staff had difficulty understanding key aspects of Madoff's fraud.[22] Similarly, a 2011 SEC IG report found that the level of communication between OCIE and Enforcement after a referral—that is, noteworthy information from an OCIE examination passed on to Enforcement for further investigation or action—was not always

---

[20]Of the staff and supervisors who responded to our survey, 32 percent had not contacted employees in the division of Corporation Finance, 40 percent had not contacted employees in Investment Management, 37 percent had not contacted employees in Trading and Markets, and 50 percent had not contacted employees in Economic and Risk Analysis. SEC employees contacted the Division of Enforcement more frequently, with 19 percent of the respondents saying that they had not contacted Enforcement. SEC officials explained that there are many projects for which communication across divisions might not be necessary, and that this is partly why a sizable percentage of employees had not contacted employees in other divisions.

[21]According to results from OPM's 2012 Federal Employee Viewpoint Survey, which surveyed employees from 82 federal agencies (constituting 97 percent of executive branch agencies), 53.3 percent of employees responding to the survey provided a positive response (agree or strongly agree) to the statement that managers promote communication among different work units, about 23.0 percent provided a neutral response (neither agree nor disagree), and 23.8 percent provided a negative response (disagree or strongly disagree).

[22]OIG-467.

consistent in the regional offices, which can hinder SEC's ability to achieve its mission.[23]

In addition, the 2011 Boston Consulting Group's report also noted that SEC's culture impaired communication and collaboration between divisions. Each division's internal structure was tailored to division-specific needs, and SEC historically placed limited emphasis on using formalized mechanisms for cross-divisional collaboration.[24] Furthermore, according to three former SEC officials, managers generally have not encouraged staff to move between divisions and work in different areas. The former officials told us that managers did not encourage staff to move around because they were afraid to lose a staff slot in their division. One former official explained that staff often were reluctant to discuss their desire to rotate among divisions because such interest might be misinterpreted as a desire to leave SEC. A compartmentalized environment could result in missed opportunities for leveraging knowledge and skills of staff across the divisions and may have contributed to past enforcement failures.

SEC's culture is hierarchical. Many current staff and two former SEC officials described the agency's culture as hierarchical. Close to 42 percent of nonsupervisory staff did not agree that they had a voice in decisions that affected them and their work environment (see table 4). One former SEC director told us that although nonsupervisory and lower-level supervisory staff might have the most knowledge of a particular matter, they did not speak out very much because staff are not encouraged to challenge ideas or challenge more senior-level staff.

---

[23]See OIG-493. According to SEC officials, SEC has addressed the recommendation in this report and now has committees for discussing referrals.

[24]See Boston Consulting Group, *U.S. Securities and Exchange Commission: Organizational Study and Reform.*

Table 4: Survey Responses from SEC Employees about Having a Voice in Decision Making, as of January-March 2013

Survey statement: *I have a voice in decisions that affect me and my work environment.*

Response category	Nonsupervisory staff	Supervisory staff	Senior officers
Strongly agree/somewhat agree	38.3%	63.1%	92.2%
Neither agree or disagree	17.9	12.1	4.7
Strongly disagree/somewhat disagree	41.8	23.6	1.6
Do not know	1.3	0.0	0.0
No response checked	0.8	1.3	1.6
Total	**100**	**100**	**100**
(number of respondents)	**(1,462)**	**(390)**	**(64)**

Source: GAO.

Note: Percentages may not always add to 100 due to rounding.

The 2011 Boston Consulting Group report also stated that, while good communication existed at the most senior level, information did not always travel down as effectively as it should. Such hierarchical culture may discourage open communication and innovation because staff may be reluctant to speak up and share ideas.

SEC culture is risk averse. Many current staff and two former officials described SEC's culture as risk averse, and some also noted that aversion to risk has grown in recent years. In our survey of SEC employees, more than half of staff (supervisory and nonsupervisory) and more than 62 percent of senior officers agreed that the fear of public scandals may have contributed to the culture of risk aversion at SEC (see table 5). For example, a few senior officers and staff surveyed remarked that recent enforcement failures and related, sustained criticism from members of Congress, SEC's former Inspector General, and the public has contributed to their unwillingness to take risks and innovate.

Table 5: Survey Responses from SEC Employees about Risk Aversion, as of January-March 2013

Survey statement: *Fear of public scandals has made SEC overly cautious and risk-averse.*

Response category	Nonsupervisory staff	Supervisory staff	Senior officers
Strongly agree/somewhat agree	54.5%	57.4%	62.5%
Neither agree or disagree	16.7	14.6	12.5
Strongly disagree/somewhat disagree	21.0	24.6	25.0
Do not know	7.5	2.3	0.0
No response checked	0.3	1.3	0.0
Total	**100**	**100**	**100**
(number of respondents)	**(1,462)**	**(390)**	**(64)**

Source: GAO.

Note: Percentages may not always add to 100 due to rounding.

Furthermore, close to half of the staff (both nonsupervisory and supervisory) agreed that the fear of being wrong has made some senior officers reluctant to take a stand on important issues (see table 6). Many current SEC staff we surveyed and two former SEC officials indicated that added layers of review—which have been added because of this fear, according to staff—not only decreased efficiency but also slowed decision making.

Table 6: Survey Responses from SEC Employees about Taking a Stand on Issues, as of January-March 2013

Survey statement: *The fear of being wrong makes senior officers in my division/office reluctant to take a stand on important issues.*

Response category	Nonsupervisory staff	Supervisory staff	Senior officers
Strongly agree/somewhat agree	46.6%	44.1%	21.9%
Neither agree or disagree	15.1	13.6	12.5
Strongly disagree/somewhat disagree	26.6	38.5	62.5
Do not know	10.9	3.6	3.1
No response checked	0.8	0.3	0.0
Total	**100**	**100**	**100**
(number of respondents)	**(1,462)**	**(390)**	**(64)**

Source: GAO.

Note: Percentages may not always add to 100 due to rounding.

A number of staff who responded to our survey provided specific instances of risk aversion. For instance, according to a few survey respondents, managers have been afraid to close cases or make decisions because senior officers want to minimize the chances that they would be criticized later. Another survey respondent added that, due to such risk aversion, cases that address evolving market practices or developments with little precedent may not be pursued.

We and others have previously reported similar results. In 2009, we found that Enforcement's internal system for case review slowed cases, created an atmosphere of fear and insecurity, and may have created incentives for staff to drop cases or narrow the scope of a review.[25] Similarly, in 2010, the SEC IG reported that the desire for Enforcement staff to avoid difficult cases was partly due to challenges in dealing with the agency's bureaucracy. According to a former SEC senior officer, the arduous process of obtaining approval to recommend an enforcement action by SEC headquarters was a factor in deciding which investigations to pursue. The IG also noted there appeared to be an increased focus on easier, "slam dunk" cases over those cases that looked to be complex and more time consuming.[26] As a result, the cases chosen for investigations may not have effectively identified potential securities violations.

As it takes years for an organization's culture to take hold, it also may take years to effect changes to that culture. Such change requires sustained efforts by senior management to address challenges related to organizational culture. We found that for organizations to successfully transform themselves, they often must change their culture fundamentally. An effective personnel management system is critical to achieving this cultural transformation.

Improving Personnel Management Is Critical for SEC's Effectiveness

SEC has not consistently or fully implemented practices for effective personnel management practices. Specifically, we found deficiencies or limitations in the areas of workforce and succession planning, performance appraisals and incentives, and communication and collaboration. SEC has taken some steps to address aspects of these deficiencies or limitations, but most of the agency's efforts are in the early stages and could be enhanced. Prioritizing and enhancing personnel management efforts are critical for SEC's ability to achieve its mission and goals. Moreover, sustained leadership and attention in these efforts

---

[25]GAO-09-358.

[26]OIG-526.

from SEC's COO could help the agency overcome the natural resistance to change, marshal the resources needed to implement change, and build and maintain an *organization-wide* commitment to new ways of doing business.[27]

SEC Lacks Comprehensive Plans to Help Ensure Its Workforce Has the Necessary Skills

SEC has not yet developed a comprehensive workforce plan. A workforce plan encompasses systematic processes for identifying and addressing the gaps between current and future workforce needs. According to OPM guidance, effective workforce plans align workforce requirements with agency strategic plans, develop a comprehensive picture of gaps in competencies and future requirements, and inform decision making about how best to structure the organization and deploy the workforce. For example, a workforce plan could provide SEC management information on the types, number, and location of supervisory and nonsupervisory staff. A plan could also help management determine the type of training and other strategies needed to close gaps, while taking into consideration factors including the ratio of management to staff, industry trends, workforce diversity, and projections of retirements.[28] Moreover, according to OPM guidance, succession planning forms an integral part of workforce planning and helps ensure an ongoing supply of qualified staff to fill leadership and other key positions.[29] In September 2012, we concluded that such a plan is essential for helping ensure that SEC has

---

[27]Based on information gathered from officials at four organizations with COO-type positions and a forum with individuals with experience in business transformation, we reported in November 2007 that a senior-level position, such as a COO, can provide sustained management attention essential for addressing key stewardship responsbilities in an integrated manner while helping to facilitate the business transformation process within an agency. Responsibilities under a COO could include, among others, strategic planning, communications and information resources management, human capital strategy, and change management. See GAO-08-34.

[28]Section 962 of Dodd Frank Act required us to review the ratio of management to staff, including whether there are "excessive" numbers of low-level, mid-level, or senior-level managers. Pub. L. No. 111-203, § 962(b)(1)(G), 124 Stat. 1376, 1909 (2010). Appendix III provides additional information on the ratio of management to staff from 2008 to 2012. In addition, the act required us to review turnover rates within SEC subunits. § 962(b)(1)(F). While staff turnover rates could be used to identify potential areas for improvement and further develop current supervisors, officials from the Merit Systems Protection Board noted that turnover was not a good indicator of poor supervision for several reasons. See appendix IV for more information.

[29]See OPM, *Workforce Planning Model.*

the right mix of talent, skills, and experience to execute its mission and goals.[30]

Key principles for effective workforce planning from our past work also has shown that it is important for agencies to ensure that their strategic workforce planning efforts (1) involve top management, staff, and other stakeholders; (2) identify the critical skills and competencies that will be needed to achieve current and future programmatic results, including evaluation of gaps; (3) develop strategies that are tailored to address skills gaps; (4) build the internal capability needed to address administrative, training, and other requirements important to support workforce planning strategies; and (5) include plans to monitor and evaluate the agency's progress toward meeting its human capital goals.[31] These findings are consistent with OPM guidance.[32]

Although SEC has not yet developed a comprehensive workforce plan, SEC's OHR has been actively working to do so.[33] In response to the Boston Consulting Group report, OHR began to identify competency gaps, which is an important step in workforce planning.[34] In late 2011, OHR completed a workforce profile that provided a snapshot of current workforce composition (including information on the number and types of mission-critical occupations, education, tenure, and supervisory status) to better understand current workload gaps and workforce availability among divisions and offices. SEC's OHR also began working with the divisions to identify skill gaps. To further assess competency gaps, in October 2012 OHR sent each division and office questionnaires to determine what new functions existed and the number of positions needed to undertake those functions. In April 2013, SEC hired a staff member with expertise in workforce planning who is to focus on workforce planning efforts. The planner is to integrate workforce data and help SEC

---

[30]GAO, *Human Capital Management: Effectively Implementing Reforms and Closing Critical Skill Gaps Are Key to Addressing Federal Workforce Challenges*, GAO-12-1023T (Washington, D.C.: Sept. 19, 2012).

[31]GAO, *Human Capital: Key Principles for Effective Workforce Planning*, GAO-04-39 (Washington, D.C.: Dec. 11, 2003).

[32]See OPM, *Workforce Planning Model*.

[33] We first recommended that SEC develop such a plan in 2001. See GAO-01-947.

[34]See Boston Consulting Group, *Organizational Study and Reform*.

effectively carry out remaining workforce planning goals. In May 2013, SEC also hired a staff member with expertise in succession planning.[35]

SEC also has initiated strategies, such as hiring and training, to close skills gaps. For example, SEC'S OHR began working with the divisions to hire staff with necessary specialized and financial industry expertise. Many SEC staff with whom we spoke in one-on-one interviews indicated that the recent actions SEC has taken helped address issues related to the competence of staff across the agency. For example, our survey showed that 86 percent of nonsupervisory staff and supervisors indicated that their division was able to attract talented and qualified staff. Additionally, the majority of nonsupervisory staff, supervisors, and senior officers who responded to our survey indicated the training they received provided them with the right skills to meet SEC's needs. Furthermore, participants in about half of our 22 focus groups said that training opportunities had increased and improved in quality. Similarly, one industry representatives with whom we spoke also told us that SEC staff generally had the right set of skills to carry out SEC's mission effectively.

SEC has also expanded developmental opportunities for staff. For instance, SEC has increased technical and developmental opportunities for nonsupervisory staff by offering leadership development courses through SEC University.[36] While all supervisors can take the core leadership courses, selected courses are made available for nonsupervisory staff to promote career development to a managerial position. SEC also has offered other tools, including a 360 degree

---

[35]As of May 2013, OHR officials told us that, in addition to acquiring a workforce and a succession planner, they also revised the responsibilities of an existing staff member to support workforce and succession planning efforts.

[36]SEC University is part of OHR and consists of three colleges. The Leadership Development College focuses on leadership and offers classes to all SEC employees. SEC University collaborates with the divisions and offices to conduct training needs assessments and develop training plans to address the identified needs.

feedback program and executive coaching service to support the development of SEC's supervisors.[37]

While SEC has taken steps towards identifying and addressing its workforce competency gaps, these efforts have not reflected all of the elements of effective workforce planning and strategies articulated in OPM guidance. During our review, OHR officials told us that the agency has not conducted a thorough analysis of its workforce to comprehensively identify competency gaps, including those related to the right mix of staff to supervisors. Without a comprehensive approach to identify these gaps, any strategies to address them will not be fully effective. As indicated in our survey, more than 50 percent of nonsupervisory staff and supervisors responded that management in their divisions could do more to address skill gaps. Moreover, some SEC staff and supervisors have raised questions about the appropriateness of the ratio of staff to managers. For instance, SEC nonsupervisory and supervisory staff with whom we spoke in the focus groups and those we surveyed expressed varying views on the ratio of staff to managers; some thought it was appropriate, others thought there were too many managers. When we asked SEC's OHR how they determined an appropriate ratio, they told us that it is dependent on the complexity of the program or activity. Historically, each division took the lead in making those types of decisions, as well as decisions related to hiring and identifying training needs.

Additionally, SEC has not developed a comprehensive management succession program to fill agency supervisory positions, contrary to regulatory requirements.[38] Specifically, it lacks a transparent process for leadership succession, including how it identifies and grooms high-potential leaders, as outlined in OPM guidance and federal regulations.[39]

---

[37]The 360 assessment tool supports leadership effectiveness by targeting areas for continued development. Through feedback from superiors, peers, and subordinates, the tool generates a comprehensive evaluation of leadership effectiveness across 24 competencies, including managing conflict, leveraging differences, decisiveness, and strategic planning. "Iconnect," implemented in late 2011, is SEC's mentoring program that offers professional networking and career development opportunities to nonsupervisory staff.

[38]OPM Succession Planning Rule, 5 C.F.R. § 412.201 (2012).

[39]Human Resources Management in Agencies, HCAAF and HCAAF Systems, Standards, and Metrics, 73 Fed. Reg. 23012, 23027 (Apr. 28, 2008) (codified at 5 C.F.R. § 250.202 (2012)).

Staff also perceived the promotion process as unfair. The development of a succession plan might help address pronounced staff dissatisfaction with the promotion process. For example, a more transparent process could enable staff to have a better understanding of how high-potential leaders from within the agency are identified and make the promotion process appear less unfair. While SEC has written selection criteria for promotion, several nonsupervisory staff with whom we spoke in one-on-one interviews and whom we surveyed viewed SEC's methods for promoting individuals to supervisory positions as unclear and potentially biased. Almost 55 percent of nonsupervisory staff responded that promotion to management was mostly based on connections that staff had with management (see table 7). In addition, participants in 7 of our 22 focus groups said that it was unclear how certain individuals were selected for promotion. We found similarities between SEC employee viewpoints and those of employees at other federal agencies. For example, according to OPM's 2012 Federal Employee Viewpoint Survey, which surveyed employees from 82 federal agencies, comprising 97 percent of the agencies in the executive branch, 33.5 percent of government employees responding to the survey agreed (or strongly agreed) that promotions in their work unit were based on merit, about 29.2 percent neither agreed nor disagreed, and 37.3 percent disagreed (or strongly disagreed).

Table 7: Survey Responses from SEC Employees about Promotion to Management, as of January-March 2013

Survey statement: *Promotion to management is mostly based on the connection that staff have with management.*[a]

Response category	Nonsupervisory staff	Supervisory staff
Strongly agree/somewhat agree	54.9%	35.6%
Neither agree or disagree	14.6	19.2
Strongly disagree/somewhat disagree	12.4	39.5
Do not know	17.6	4.9
No response checked	0.6	0.8
Total	**100**	**100**
(number of respondents)	**(1,462)**	**(390)**

Source: GAO.

[a]This question was not included in the survey to senior officers.

Note: Percentages may not always add to 100 due to rounding.

Additionally, many staff we surveyed and with whom we spoke in one-on-one interviews also did not think there was much incentive to be promoted into management positions. For example, slightly more than half of nonsupervisory staff and almost 75 percent of supervisors who responded to our survey indicated that there was not much incentive to be promoted because the salary increase would be minimal (see table 8). Staff in 7 of the 22 groups said staff had little incentive to become managers because the differences in pay were minimal. Similarly, 1 in 10 staff with whom we met individually said there were no financial incentives to apply for a promotion to the first-level supervisor position. Senior officers had mixed views about the incentives for promotion. According to OHR officials, the pay differential (traditionally, 6 percent) between nonmanagers and managers has been eroded and in some cases eliminated. Because of the federal pay freeze, while nonmanagers have received merit increases every year, managers have not received any increases.

Table 8: Survey Responses from SEC Employees about Incentives for Promotion, as of January-March 2013

Survey statement: *There is not much incentive to get promoted into a management position because the salary increase is minimal.*

Response category	Nonsupervisory staff	Supervisory staff	Senior officers
Strongly agree/somewhat agree	51.6%	74.1%	42.2%
Neither agree or disagree	16.8	6.7	10.9
Strongly disagree/somewhat disagree	20.3	17.2	42.2
Do not know	10.9	1.3	3.1
No response checked	0.3	0.8	1.6
Total	**100**	**100**	**100**
(number of respondents)	**(1,462)**	**(390)**	**(63)**

Source: GAO.

Note: Percentages may not always add to 100 due to rounding.

Until SEC completes a comprehensive workforce plan, the agency will be limited in its ability to meet its workforce needs. According to agency officials, SEC has been slow to adopt comprehensive workforce planning because human capital planning has not been considered an area of high priority. OHR officials explained that SEC priorities were concentrated on mission-critical functions and, as such, OHR focused on fulfilling and complying with essential OPM reporting requirements because of resource constraints. Additionally, OHR officials noted that, prior to the recent release of SEC's first human capital strategic plan in 2012, human capital efforts generally were loosely put together and not formally linked to SEC's overall strategic plan. Our previous work has shown that sustained leadership attention by the COO or other officials will be important to address these concerns.[40] Without comprehensive workforce and succession plans, SEC will be limited in its ability to make well-informed decisions about how to best meet agency needs today and into the future.

Implementation of SEC's Performance Management System Could Be Improved

The design of SEC's performance management system reflects some characteristics of an effective system but could be improved. According to OPM guidance (primarily HCAAF) and our past work, an effective performance management system typically encompasses expectations that are set for staff, monitoring of staff's work that results in performance appraisals, feedback to staff on their performance and ways to improve it, and recognition of staff's contributions.[41] More specifically, effective performance management systems include:

- performance appraisals that distinguish between levels of performance and reward strong performance,
- meaningful and timely feedback discussions,
- actions to address poor performance,
- mechanisms to ensure supervisors properly use the system, and
- periodic staff validation of the system to ensure its credibility.

SEC's performance management system includes an appraisal system that consists of ratings designed to differentiate between levels of performance. The performance management system also requires supervisors and senior officers to use performance results to offer feedback, identify developmental needs, and address instances of poor performance. The system also includes steps and actions to address poor performance.

However, our work, as well as outside studies, suggests that SEC's implementation of its performance management system could be

---

[40] GAO-08-34.

[41] In addition to HCAAF, see OPM, *A Handbook for Measuring Employee Performance*, (Washington, D.C.: September 2011). For a list of internal safeguards key to successful implementation of performance management systems that we have previously identified, see GAO, *Human Capital: DOD Needs to Improve Implementation of and Address Employee Concerns about its National Security Personnel System*, GAO-08-773 (Washington, D.C.: Sept. 10, 2008).

improved. SEC staff expressed many concerns about the implementation of the performance management system. For example, staff expressed concerns about the link between their performance and ratings, limited performance incentives, unconstructive feedback, and the extent of actions taken to address poor performance. SEC senior officers expressed concerns about the system as well. By not addressing these implementation concerns, the agency could face challenges in retaining a high-quality workforce that is actively engaged in the work of SEC, which in turn, could affect the agency's ability to adequately carry out its mission.

Performance Appraisal System and Incentives

According to HCAAF, an effective performance management system distinguishes between levels of performance and rewards strong performance. Although the design of SEC's performance appraisal system reflects these elements, SEC staff raised a number of concerns related to how the appraisal system is applied, and the link between their performance and incentives (that is, pay and rewards). Our survey results revealed that about 43 percent of nonsupervisory staff did not believe their performance appraisals are fair and appropriate (see table 9). Similarly, participants in the majority of the focus groups we conducted with nonsupervisory staff stated that their ratings were arbitrary and not meaningful, and that their ratings under the current appraisal system did not fully reflect their accomplishments. In contrast, most supervisors and senior officers that responded to our survey indicated that they thought staff performance appraisals were fair and appropriate.

Table 9: Survey Responses from SEC Employees about Fairness and Appropriateness of Performance Appraisals, as of January-March 2013

Survey statement: *Employee performance appraisals are fair and appropriate under SEC's performance management system.*

Response category	Nonsupervisory staff	Supervisory staff	Senior officers
Strongly agree/somewhat agree	20.1%	51.8%	70.3%
Neither agree or disagree	21.0	18.5	17.2
Strongly disagree/somewhat disagree	42.8	26.9	10.9
Do not know	14.8	1.5	0
No response checked	1.2	1.3	1.6
Total	**100**	**100**	**100**
(number of respondents)	**(1,462)**	**(390)**	**(64)**

Source: GAO.

Note: Percentages may not always add to 100 due to rounding.

A 2012 study of SEC's performance management system, conducted by an independent third party, found similar results.[42] Specifically, almost half of the nonsupervisory staff that responded to that study's survey indicated that their appraisal rating did not accurately reflect their performance. We compared SEC employee viewpoints from our survey to those of employees at other federal agencies and identified differences. According to OPM's 2012 Federal Employee Viewpoint Survey, about 16 percent of employees government-wide responding to the survey disagreed (or strongly disagreed) that their performance appraisal was a fair reflection of their performance.

Staff also raised concerns about whether the system, as implemented, rewarded strong performance. A little more than one-third of nonsupervisory SEC staff who responded to our survey indicated that there was a clear link between their performance and recognition of it; about the same amount said that a clear link did not exist (see table 10).

Table 10: Survey Responses from SEC Employees about Performance and Recognition, as of January-March 2013

Survey statement: *There is a clear link between my performance and recognition of it.*

Response category	Nonsupervisory staff	Supervisory staff	Senior officers
Strongly agree/somewhat agree	37.6%	60.5%	59.4%
Neither agree or disagree	17.4	14.1	20.3
Strongly disagree/somewhat disagree	38.6	24.6	18.8
Do not know	5.5	0	0
No response checked	1.0	0.8	1.6
Total	**100**	**100**	**100**
(number of respondents)	**(1,462)**	**(390)**	**(64)**

Source: GAO.

Note: Percentages may not always add to 100 due to rounding.

---

[42] In March 2011, SEC and the SEC employees' union agreed to have an independent, third party conduct a study of the application of the performance management system for fiscal year 2011, which was completed in 2012. See, Robert Tobias, *Evaluation of the U.S. Securities and Exchange Commission's Evidence Based Performance Management System* (Washington, D.C.: June 1, 2012). The Tobias study included a survey made available to all SEC employees and advertised in the *SEC Today* newsletter. The survey received 1,387 responses (77 percent bargaining unit; 11 percent nonbargaining unit/nonsupervisory; and 13 percent management/supervisory). This equated to a response rate of approximately 39 percent.

We also heard concerns related to the link between performance and pay from staff in our focus groups. According to nonsupervisory and supervisory staff in 17 of the 22 focus groups we conducted, the performance appraisal process was not meaningful, as bargaining unit staff who received an acceptable rating received the same pay increase (measured in percentage) regardless of the rating score. OHR officials acknowledged that all bargaining unit staff across SEC that received an acceptable rating received the same pay increase (percentage) during fiscal year 2012. According to these officials, SEC has not been able to implement the pay-for-performance element of the system because negotiations with the employees' union remain ongoing. Such across-the-board pay increases weaken the link between pay and performance. In contrast, SEC has put in place pay-for-performance for supervisors and senior officers. Most supervisors (almost 61 percent) and senior officers (almost 60 percent) who responded to our survey said a clear link existed between their performance and recognition of it.

Staff also expressed concerns with the awards process. SEC has an awards program that is designed to recognize employee contributions above and beyond normal job requirements and provide monetary and nonmonetary awards.[43] However, more than 60 percent of nonsupervisory staff and about 43 percent of supervisory staff who responded to our survey indicated that they did not think the criteria for rewarding staff were clearly defined. In addition, staff in the majority of nonsupervisory focus groups we conducted asserted that the awards process was not transparent. For example, staff told us that it was unclear what was required to receive an award for strong performance and why some staff received awards and others did not. Senior officers with whom we spoke in one division had similar perspectives and stated that the criteria and tasks associated with different levels of awards were not sufficiently transparent. In some of the focus groups we conducted, SEC staff also told us that the awards themselves, partly due to budget constraints, were not particularly meaningful. Some supervisors also commented that they had few means to motivate staff.

---

[43]SEC has a separate awards program, albeit limited due to budget constraints, for strong performance. The program is designed to motivate employees and recognize contributions above and beyond normal job requirements, and includes monetary and nonmonetary awards. SEC's Office of Human Resources (OHR) is responsible for monitoring and evaluating documentation for award recommendations, and the use of approval authority for awards that OHR delegated to divisions.

GAO-13-621 SEC Personnel Management

Feedback

According to OPM guidance, an effective performance management system requires and encourages meaningful feedback discussions. Moreover, it states that meaningful feedback provides opportunities for supervisors to offer specific details on staff's performance and suggestions on how staff can improve certain aspects of his/her performance. SEC requires supervisors and managers to conduct a formal feedback meeting at the end of the performance cycle and to provide feedback to each of their staff on their performance that is specific, descriptive, and objective. SEC also encourages supervisors and managers to solicit questions from staff during performance feedback session.

The majority of SEC nonsupervisory and supervisory staff are generally satisfied with the feedback they received. According to our survey of nonsupervisory and supervisory staff, the majority of respondents indicated that they received useful feedback from their direct supervisors (see table 11).

Table 11: Survey Responses from SEC Employees about Feedback from Direct Supervisors, as of January-March 2013

Survey statement: *My direct supervisor provides useful and constructive feedback.*[a]

Response category	Nonsupervisory staff	Supervisory staff
Strongly agree/somewhat agree	65.3%	70.5%
Neither agree or disagree	11.9	9.5
Strongly disagree/somewhat disagree	20.1	16.7
Do not know	1.0	1.0
No response checked	1.6	2.3
Total	**100**	**100**
(number of respondents)	**(1,462)**	**(390)**

Source: GAO.

[a]This question was not included in the survey to senior officers.

Note: Percentages may not always add to 100 due to rounding.

However, some nonsupervisory staff raised concerns about the quality of the feedback they received. About 20 percent of nonsupervisory staff that responded to our survey indicated that they did not receive useful or constructive feedback. Among these respondents, some commented that the feedback was vague or did not provide specific suggestions for improvement. Similarly, some staff in our focus groups said that they did not receive meaningful feedback. We found similarities between SEC employee viewpoints and those of employees at other federal agencies.[44] However, in the 2012 third-party study, nearly half of SEC employees who completed the survey indicated that they had not received meaningful feedback from their supervisors, and the study found that about a quarter of the respondents did not indicate that they had a formal feedback session during the annual rating period when the survey was conducted.[45] In focus groups and interviews we conducted with nonsupervisory and supervisory staff, timeliness was generally not identified as an issue related to feedback.

SEC has taken steps to address some staff's concerns about feedback. For example, SEC has provided training to supervisors on how to provide clear performance expectations and effectively counsel staff on their performance. However, implementing mechanisms to monitor supervisors' efforts to provide meaningful feedback could provide SEC with greater assurance that its supervisors are providing feedback to staff as intended and that staff have the information to maintain or adjust their performance accordingly.

Actions to Address Staff Performance

OPM guidance states that an effective performance management system outlines actions that supervisors should take to address staff performance and, in particular, staff who are not meeting performance expectations. Such actions are important because they attempt to rectify poor performance that could be affecting an agency's ability to achieve its mission or goals. SEC's system includes a process to address poor performing staff. Specifically, those who receive an overall rating of unacceptable are placed on a performance improvement plan that requires them to meet certain goals to demonstrate improvement. To complete the improvement plan, staff must maintain the improved level of performance for the duration of the plan. If staff do not improve and

---

[44]According to results from OPM's 2012 Federal Employee Viewpoint Survey, which surveyed employees from 82 federal agencies (comprising 97 percent of executive branch agencies), about 61 percent of employees responding to the survey agreed (or strongly agreed) that their supervisors or team leaders provided constructive suggestions to improve their job performance, about 21 percent neither agreed nor disagreed, and about 19 percent disagreed (or strongly disagreed). Percentages do not add up to 100 due to rounding.

[45]Tobias, *Evaluation of the U.S. Securities and Exchange Commission's Evidence Based Performance Management System.*

sustain performance at an acceptable level during the duration of the plan, SEC can demote or dismiss the staff.

Although SEC's performance management system includes such elements, employees reported concerns about how SEC addressed poor performing supervisors and staff.

- **Poor performing supervisors.** According to the results from our survey, staff generally do not think SEC senior officers or supervisors effectively deal with poor performers. About 56 percent of the nonsupervisory staff and about 47 percent of supervisory staff who responded to our survey indicated that senior officers do not deal effectively with poor performing supervisors (see table 12). Similarly, in about one-third of our focus groups, nonsupervisory staff and supervisors both stated that SEC generally had not taken actions against poor supervisors. In contrast, a little more than half of the senior officers who responded to our survey reported that they dealt effectively with poor-performing supervisors.

Table 12: Survey Responses from SEC Employees about How Senior Officers Dealt with Poorly Performing Supervisors, as of January-March 2013

Survey statement: *Overall, senior officers deal effectively with poor-performing supervisors and managers.*			
Response category	Nonsupervisory staff	Supervisory staff	Senior officers
Strongly agree/somewhat agree	5.3%	24.9%	56.3%
Neither agree or disagree	9.9	15.1	17.2
Strongly disagree/somewhat disagree	56.2	46.7	23.4
Do not know	28.4	13.3	3.1
No response checked	0.1	0	0
Total (number of respondents)	**100** (1,462)	**100** (390)	**100** (64)

Source: GAO.

Note: Percentages may not always add to 100 due to rounding.

- **Poor performing staff.** More than 50 percent of both nonsupervisory staff and supervisors who responded to our survey indicated that supervisors did not deal effectively with poorly performing staff (see table 13). Some supervisors commented that dealing with poor-performing staff often is very time-consuming. Similarly, according to results from OPM's 2012 Federal Employee Viewpoint Survey, 43 percent of employees government-wide responding to the survey disagreed (or strongly disagreed) that in their work unit, steps were taken to deal with a poor performer who could not or would not improve.

Table 13: Survey Responses from SEC Employees about How Supervisors Dealt with Poorly Performing Staff, as of January-March 2013

Survey statement: *Overall, supervisors and managers deal effectively with poor-performing staff.*[a]

Response category	Nonsupervisory staff	Supervisory staff
Strongly agree/somewhat agree	9.6%	28.5%
Neither agree or disagree	12.4	12.8
Strongly disagree/somewhat disagree	51.1	55.1
Do not know	26.6	3.1
No response checked	0.3	0.5
Total	**100**	**100**
(number of respondents)	**(1,462)**	**(390)**

Source: GAO.

[a]This question was not included in the survey to senior officers.

When we spoke to OHR officials about how SEC has dealt with poor performing staff, they told us that actions taken against poor performing staff are confidential and, as a result, SEC staff may not be aware of how poor performance has been addressed. According to OHR officials, from 2007 through June 2013, SEC placed 38 staff under performance improvement plans. Subsequently, 2 staff were terminated, 10 resigned, 3 were reassigned within SEC, 18 successfully completed the improvement plan, 1 has a proposed removal pending, and 4 are still in the performance improvement plan period as of June 2013.[46]

Mechanisms to Monitor Supervisors' Use of the Performance Management System

According to OPM guidance, an effective performance management system monitors how supervisors use the system and provide feedback to staff, includes performance standards for supervisors in these areas, and requires that supervisors' performance in these areas be part of their

---

[46]During the same period, SEC took one adverse action (which is separate from the improvement plan process and can include unpaid suspension, demotion, or removal) against an employee for poor performance. The adverse action resulted in the resignation of the employee in lieu of termination. Regarding actions taken against poor performing employees, we do not have similar information for other federal agencies so we could not determine how SEC's removal rates compare to those of other federal agencies.

feedback and performance evaluations. Without such mechanisms, it is more difficult to ensure accountability in how aspects of the performance management system are applied, especially the performance appraisal process whereby supervisors assess a subordinate's performance, develop a corresponding rating, recognize their performance, and deliver feedback to the subordinate about his or her performance.

While SEC has performance standards related to supervisors' use of the performance management system, we did not identify specific mechanisms for how SEC monitors supervisors' use of the system. For example, while staff have the option to prepare written narratives on how they assess their own performance for that rating period, we did not identify mechanisms that monitor how supervisors use information from staff narratives to help ensure they prepare complete and accurate appraisal ratings for staff. Senior officers in the six divisions told us they reviewed narratives that supervisors wrote to support a subordinate's rating for the purpose of ensuring that the narrative supported the rating. However, this only serves to ensure that the narrative supports a rating, and not that the rating itself is an accurate representation of the subordinate's performance. For example, consistent with OPM guidance, senior officers could assess how well supervisors monitor and assess staff performance by comparing the summaries that staff prepare assessing their own work against the ratings that supervisors prepare for these staff. Moreover, we found that some supervisors with whom we spoke have had limited discussions with their own supervisors about how they use the system to recognize and reward strong staff performance, provide feedback to staff, or take actions to deal with poor performance.

Without such mechanisms, there is an increased risk that accountability for performance appraisal processes and activities—such as developing ratings and delivering feedback—will be diminished. Mechanisms that monitor how the system is being applied and used by supervisors, such as ongoing feedback conversations between supervisors and their superiors, could help ensure that staff are receiving appraisals that reflect all of their performance during the rating period, are being provided meaningful feedback, and that poor performance is addressed in a timely and effective manner. Sustained management attention would help encourage the development of such mechanisms.

Validation of System	We previously concluded that an effective performance management system includes periodic validation of the system to help ensure its credibility.[47] Validating the system typically refers to obtaining staff input and general agreement on the competencies, rating procedures, and other aspects of the system.

SEC has taken some steps to obtain staff input on a portion of its performance management system. Specifically, SEC sought staff input on the creation of the performance standards for various occupations, including attorneys and examiners. However, managers validated and finalized these performance standards. Furthermore, we could not identify additional SEC efforts to obtain staff input on other aspects of its performance management system, such as the performance appraisal process. The safeguards that we previously identified are key to successful implementation of performance management systems in the federal government. We identified these safeguards based on our work looking at the performance management practices used by leading public sector organizations in the United States and in other countries, as well as our experiences in implementing a modern performance management system for our own staff at GAO. Among these safeguards, we've stated that it is vital for agencies to directly involve staff in the implementation of all aspects of a performance management system. According to OHR officials, they plan to validate the performance management system once SEC and the union reach agreement on the revisions currently being negotiated, but it is unclear when they will reach agreement since they have been in negotiations for several years. Validating the performance management system with staff input on aspects beyond performance standards and objectives could help enhance the credibility of SEC's performance management system among its staff, including the ratings, recognition, or feedback that they receive as a result.

SEC Has Yet to Fully Address Barriers to Communication and Collaboration

Although SEC has improved intra-agency communication and collaboration, barriers still exist. As discussed previously in this report, current and former SEC staff and others use words like "siloed communication" and "hierarchical" to describe SEC's culture. Such an environment can hinder SEC's ability to effectively carry out its mission by limiting communication and collaboration among the divisions. For

---

[47]GAO-08-773.

example, as noted earlier in this report, SEC's IG has reported on how this lack of communication and collaboration may have contributed to past enforcement failures.

According to HCAAF, supervisors and managers should foster an environment of open communication. Such communication, as found in our previous work, can facilitate a collaborative environment, enable more efficient work processes, and prevent misunderstandings. Open and effective communication occurs when information flows down, across, and up the organization. Frequent communication among collaborating divisions within an agency provides a means by which to facilitate working across intra-agency boundaries.[48] In prior work, we identified practices that can help to enhance and sustain collaboration among federal agencies, which can help to maximize performance and results, and have recommended that agencies follow them. These collaborative practices include identifying common outcomes, establishing joint strategies, leveraging resources, determining roles and responsibilities, and developing compatible policies and procedures, among others.

SEC has taken some steps to address its communication challenges and enhance collaboration within and among divisions.

- Enforcement created national specialized units to focus its investigations on high-priority areas such as asset management, market abuse, and structured and new products in August 2009. The specialized units work with OCIE and other divisions to identify high-risk areas for further examination and investigation. Over the last year, Enforcement also has taken steps to improve headquarters interactions, including developing guidelines for the role of trial counsel in investigations and investigative staff in litigated matters. The division also formed an advisory committee, which according to SEC officials includes supervisors and managers, to identify broader cultural or structural reforms to improve coordination.

---

[48]We reviewed program areas among select federal agencies that have demonstrated a sustained effort to collaborate within and among agencies and identified key principles that they consistently applied, such as, frequent communication to facilitate working across agency and office boundaries. GAO, *Results-Oriented Government: Practices That Can Help Enhance and Sustain Collaboration among Federal Agencies*, GAO-06-15 (Washington, D.C.: Oct. 21, 2005); and *Managing For Results: Key Considerations for Implementing Interagency Collaborative Mechanisms*, GAO-12-1022 (Washington, D.C.: Sept. 27, 2012).

- OCIE created the National Examination Program (NEP) in 2010 to emphasize intra-agency collaboration and increase communication among different regional offices and divisions. OCIE established a standardized set of policies and procedures for conducting examinations under NEP to enhance coordinated examination and inspection activities. OCIE also established regular monthly national teleconferences of examiners across regions and headquarters, developed new processes for communicating with Enforcement about new and pending examination referrals, and set mutual goals with other divisions.
- Several divisions also created new offices or subunits to help facilitate communication and collaboration with other divisions. For example, according to SEC officials, OCIE, Enforcement, and Investment Management hired new communication managers in fiscal year 2013 to develop more robust internal communication within their programs.
- In January 2013, SEC's Office of Public Affairs established a cross-divisional internal communications working group to help ensure that appropriate attention is given to internal communication within the agency.

Both SEC staff and external stakeholders have started to see some positive effects from the recent efforts to bolster communication and collaboration. For example, when asked whether communication between divisions on work-related matters was encouraged, about 54 percent of nonsupervisory staff, 75 percent of supervisors, and 94 percent of senior officers strongly or somewhat agreed that such communication was encouraged. When asked about the effects of these recent efforts, specifically those that senior officers were making to improve communication and collaboration between divisions, many staff viewed these efforts as positive. For example, nonsupervisory staff (38 percent) and many supervisors (62 percent) thought that senior officers were making a moderate to great effort to improve collaboration among divisions.[49] Representatives from one of the industry groups with whom we spoke said recent improvements in coordination across SEC's regional offices has reduced the duplicative efforts that in the past incurred unnecessary time and money. The representatives also noted

---

[49]Our survey results are generally consistent with OPM's 2012 Federal Employee Viewpoint Survey of federal agencies, in which slightly more than half of employees government-wide responding to the survey agreed (or strongly agreed) that managers supported collaboration and communication across units.

that in meetings with SEC, multiple SEC divisions often have been represented.

Although the agency has taken efforts to improve its intra-agency communication and collaboration, staff continued to identify barriers to effective communication and collaboration among the divisions, within divisions, and between staff and management, contrary to collaborative best practices. For example, many nonsupervisory staff and supervisors who responded to our survey commented on communication issues and challenges, such as that they were frustrated that relevant and timely information was not freely communicated across units because of the need to obtain management approval to share such information. Rather than leveraging resources, according to some staff, various divisions function as individual "fiefdoms." Former senior SEC officials with whom we spoke individually explained that some supervisors and senior officers felt the need to protect their "turf" and status in the agency by not sharing information. Furthermore, representatives from SEC's union told us that management frowned on communication across divisions without going through formal channels. As noted earlier, about one-third of the SEC staff who responded to our survey said they had not contacted staff in other divisions (outside of Enforcement) over the last year on work-related matters, such as coordinating activities or seeking expert advice. But, according to senior officers with whom we spoke from multiple divisions, cross-division communication and collaboration may not be necessary in many instances. They told us that staff involved in rulemaking are concentrated in a relatively small group of individuals, and staff in similar specialized roles may have fewer work-related opportunities or reasons to reach out across the agency for expertise or to coordinate work.

SEC staff also said barriers to communication and collaboration among offices in the same division exist. For example, they identified working relationships between investigative and trial attorneys in headquarters as a challenge. Senior officers in Enforcement told us in an interview that investigative attorneys in headquarters end their involvement in a matter once they complete their investigation and hand it off to the trial unit for prosecution. Further, the two units report to different supervisors and are located in different physical spaces, leading to inefficiencies due to a lack of continuity and collaboration, which are essential when building and prosecuting cases. For example, a trial attorney told us that there are times when the evidence that the investigative attorneys produce is not sufficient to successfully try a case and as a result they either have to gather additional evidence, or they choose not to pursue the case and waste the past efforts of the investigators. This process is inconsistent with best practices related to intra-agency collaboration—such as identifying joint strategies designed to help align different division and subdivision activities and resources with the aim of achieving a common outcome. In contrast, investigative and trial attorneys in the regional offices work together collaboratively throughout the investigation and trial phases. Both units report to the same supervisor and are co-located. According to staff, reporting to the same supervisor and being co-located helps the attorneys to stay in constant communication and collaborate from the beginning to the end of a case, facilitating their work.

Concerns were also raised about the nature of communication between managers and staff. Nonsupervisory staff were divided about whether supervisors included staff in the flow of relevant information, but the majority of supervisors thought they effectively included staff in the flow of information (see table 14). Many nonsupervisory staff and supervisors who responded to our survey commented that they were frustrated that relevant and timely information was not freely communicated among higher- and lower-level staff. For instance, several commented that the downward flow of information was nearly nonexistent or filtered, while upward flow (particularly staff suggestions to management) was not encouraged.[50] Some nonsupervisory staff with whom we spoke characterized this as senior officers and supervisors "controlling" the flow of information.

---

[50]Two hundred and fifty-eight of 2,439 SEC staff responded to our open-ended questions in the section on communication. Of those who provided written comments, the top three response categories were communication between divisions/offices (39.5 percent), communication within divisions/offices (21.7 percent), and communication that is hierarchical (top to bottom) or not free flowing (13.2 percent).

GAO-13-621 SEC Personnel Management

Table 14: Survey Responses from SEC Employees about Flow of Relevant Information, as of January-March 2013

Survey statement: *Supervisors and managers ensure that employees are included in the flow of relevant information.*[a]

Response category	Nonsupervisory staff	Supervisory staff
Strongly agree/somewhat agree	47.7%	73.1%
Neither agree or disagree	11.6	7.9
Strongly disagree/somewhat disagree	39.0	19.0
Do not know	1.3	0
No response checked	0.3	0
Total	**100**	**100**
(number of respondents)	**(1,462)**	**(390)**

Source: GAO.

[a]This question was not included in the survey to senior officers.

Note: Percentages may not always add to 100 due to rounding.

Staff views again were divided about support for two-way communication. As shown in table 15, about half of the nonsupervisory and supervisory staff indicated their divisions supported open and two-way communication between staff and management. Roughly one-third of staff indicated that their divisions did not support such communication. During our review, we did not identify any steps that SEC has taken to systematically address challenges associated with two-way communication between staff and management.

Table 15: Survey Responses from SEC Employees about Open Communication between Staff and Management, as of January-March 2013

Survey statement: *My division/office supports open, two-way communication between staff and management.*

Response category	Nonsupervisory staff	Supervisory staff	Senior officers
Strongly agree/somewhat agree	49.5	55.1	93.8
Neither agree or disagree	13.5	14.1	4.7
Strongly disagree/somewhat disagree	35.4	29.0	1.6
Do not know	0.9	0.5	0
No response checked	0.6	1.3	0
Total	**100**	**100**	**100**
(number of respondents)	**(1,462)**	**(390)**	**(64)**

Source: GAO.

Note: Percentages may not always add to 100 due to rounding.

Despite recent efforts to break down silos, we found that they continue to exist, and communication between staff and management still tends to be top-down. Such an environment can hinder SEC's ability to effectively carry out its mission by limiting communication and leading collaboration practices. Without a sustained management focus on implementing leading communication and collaboration practices, SEC continues to face increased risks of inefficiencies and less-than-optimal decision making about its market oversight, investigative, and enforcement functions. SEC can also foster and encourage more communication and collaboration among its staff by, for example, setting formal expectations for its supervisors to foster an environment of communication and collaboration, as well as recognizing exceptional teamwork, which it currently does not. These efforts would be consistent with OPM guidance in recognizing and rewarding an environment of teamwork.[51]

SEC Has Not Developed a System to Monitor and Evaluate Its Personnel Management Activities

SEC has not developed an accountability system to monitor and evaluate its personnel management programs and systems (such as its workforce and succession planning functions and performance appraisal system). According to HCAAF, an accountability system is intended to evaluate results and provide consistent means for an agency to monitor and analyze its performance on all aspects of human capital management policies, programs, and systems.

The accountability system also contributes to an agency's performance by identifying and monitoring necessary improvements. The accountability system should provide for annual assessments of an agency's progress and results related to human capital management. The results should inform an agency's human capital goals and objectives, in conjunction with strategic planning and performance budgets. Moreover, OPM officials also explained that the accountability system is an integral part of an evaluation system that OPM uses to determine how well agencies are monitoring and evaluating their human capital activities and programs.

According to OHR officials, human capital functions at SEC had not been a priority until 2009. As a result, limited resources had been allocated to

---

[51]Capital Assessment and Accountability Framework (HCAAF) and HCAAF Systems, Standards, and Metrics, 73 Fed. Reg. 23012, 23029 (Apr. 28, 2008) (codified at 5 C.F.R. § 250.202 (2012)).

human capital functions, such as the development of an accountability system. However, SEC's OHR officials said they have been developing such a system, and noted that implementing this comprehensive system would be a multiyear project. However, during our audit, OHR officials did not provide us with any specific documentation on the development of the system, how it will be implemented, and what steps will be taken to ensure its completion. In commenting on a draft of this report, SEC stated that they have recently developed milestones and deliverables for the implementation of the system, which SEC anticipates will be fully implemented by the end of this calendar year. Until a system is put into place, SEC may be missing opportunities to take a more comprehensive approach to improving its personnel management. Moreover, without the information such a system generates, it will be difficult for SEC to identify systemic problems related to its personnel management or to correct them.

Conclusions

Maintaining a top-notch, high-performing workforce is critical to SEC effectively carrying out its existing and new regulatory responsibilities in increasingly complex markets. However, SEC's organizational culture has not been conducive to motivating and encouraging a high level of performance—many staff indicated that morale is low and a significant percentage characterize the atmosphere of the agency as one of distrust. Successfully transforming organizational culture requires an effective personnel management system. While personnel management traditionally has not been a priority at SEC, the agency has placed a new emphasis on it. However, continued work—and sustained leadership attention—would help to address a number of personnel management issues.

First, SEC lacks planning mechanisms to guide decision making about the appropriate number and skill mix of staff and does not have a transparent process to identify and develop potential leaders for future needs. OPM guidance outlines elements of effective workforce and succession plans, including action plans that help agencies move forward expeditiously and maintain a focus on developing leaders with the necessary managerial skills to effectively manage the agency's workforce. SEC is developing workforce and succession plans, but has been slow to adopt such plans. Developing workforce and succession plans in line with OPM guidance would help ensure that SEC's planning efforts were comprehensive, systematic, and forward looking and focused on obtaining, training, and retaining the workforce and leadership to help the agency achieve its mission.

Second, nonsupervisory and supervisory staff perceptions about SEC's performance appraisal system were broadly negative—many staff viewed the way that the system was used as arbitrary and ineffective and some supervisors expressed concern about the system lacking meaningful incentives for strong performance. While SEC's performance appraisal system reflects many elements of OPM guidance, no system, regardless of how well it is designed, will meet its intended purpose if it is not implemented well. SEC's implementation of its performance management system could be improved by creating ways to monitor how supervisors use the system to recognize and reward performance, provide meaningful feedback, and effectively address poor performers and by conducting periodic validations with staff input (and making changes, as appropriate), consistent with key principles identified in our past work. Although developing a performance appraisal system that is appreciated by all SEC staff should not be the goal of SEC's efforts, developing and implementing a system that is credible is critical. Without a credible system, its value and merit will continue to be questioned.

Third, while SEC has taken steps towards improving intra-agency communication, roughly one-third of staff indicated that their divisions did not support two-way communication between staff and management. Because these are long-standing concerns, sustained leadership to improve communication and collaboration within SEC is important and exploring and implementing leading communication and collaboration practices could better position SEC to address these issues. We previously reported that top leadership attention of a COO could build and maintain an *organization-wide* commitment to new ways of doing business. Furthermore, SEC could implement incentives for all staff to foster open communication and collaboration as well as hold them accountable for doing so. For example, SEC could recognize exceptional teamwork efforts through special awards and set formal expectations of its supervisors to foster an environment of communication and collaboration. By enhancing its ongoing efforts and taking more steps to improve intra-agency communication throughout the agency, SEC can improve operations and address widely held views of the agency as "siloed" and "hierarchical."

Finally, SEC has not yet implemented a system to continually monitor and evaluate its personnel management system—the activities, policies, and programs that include its workforce planning efforts and performance appraisal system. According to OPM guidance, such routine monitoring and evaluation enables agencies to refine and adjust their approaches to help ensure the ongoing effectiveness of personnel management activities. SEC has started work to develop an accountability system. Prioritizing the development of such a system and ensuring that it is consistent with HCAAF guidance and standards would put SEC firmly on a path to better plan, sustain, and refine its personnel management strategies over the long term.

Recommendations for Executive Action

To help SEC address identified personnel management challenges, the Chairman should take the following seven actions.

To enhance SEC's ability to strategically hire and retain the appropriate number of staff with the requisite skill sets for today and in the future, the Chairman of SEC should direct the COO and OHR to

- prioritize efforts to expeditiously develop a comprehensive workforce plan, including a succession plan, and establish time frames for implementation and mechanisms to help ensure that the plans are regularly updated; and
- incorporate OPM guidance as it develops its workforce and succession plans, by developing a formal action plan to identify and close competency gaps, and fill supervisory positions; and institute a fair and transparent process for identifying high-potential leaders from within the agency.

To help enhance the credibility of its performance management system, the Chairman of SEC should direct the COO and OHR to

- create mechanisms to monitor how supervisors use the performance management system to recognize and reward performance, provide meaningful feedback to staff, and effectively address poor performance; for example, by requiring ongoing feedback discussions with higher-level supervisors; and
- conduct periodic validations (with staff input) of the performance management system and make changes, as appropriate, based on these validations.

To build on SEC's efforts to enhance intra-agency communication and collaboration, the Chairman should direct the COO to

- identify and implement incentives for all staff to support an environment of open communication and collaboration, such as setting formal expectations for its supervisors to foster such an environment, and recognizing and awarding exceptional teamwork efforts; and

- explore communication and collaboration best practices and implement those that could benefit SEC.

Finally, to increase accountability of SEC's personnel management system, the Chairman of SEC should direct the COO and OHR to

- prioritize and expedite efforts to develop and implement a system to monitor and evaluate personnel management activities, policies, and programs, including establishing and documenting the steps necessary to ensure completion of the system.

Agency Comments

We provided SEC a draft copy of this report for review and comment. SEC provided written comments that are reprinted in appendix V. In written comments, SEC agreed with our recommendations. SEC acknowledged that improvements could be made in SEC's personnel management and noted that our report contained useful information that will help the agency strengthen personnel management. The letter also stated that SEC was committed to investing the time and resources to improve its organizational culture and personnel management. For example, as we noted in our report, SEC plans to improve its ability to identify and address workforce competency gaps through its newly established workforce and succession planning function. Three staff members will coordinate all workforce succession planning agency-wide. In addition, the letter noted that SEC recently implemented pay-for-performance for nonbargaining unit employees, would assess the impact of the system on those employees, and offer additional training to managers. SEC also agreed that interagency communication and collaboration remained challenges, but said these issues were a top priority and SEC would continue to leverage the results from the steps it is taking to improve in this area. For example, SEC indicated that OCIE has recently formed nine specialized working groups, involving over 600 staff from across the agency, to facilitate the sharing of information on key risk areas and industry trends. SEC also stated that it has recently added an Assistant Regional Director of Operations position in each regional office to help facilitate communication and ensure consistency across the agency. Finally, SEC described its most recent progress—developing key milestones and deliverables—in implementing an accountability system and to monitor and evaluate the personnel management system by the end of this calendar year. SEC anticipated that the system would address the concerns we cited in this report about aligning human capital practices and strategic goals. We updated our report to reflect SEC's recent progress on this issue.

We are sending copies of this report to interested congressional committees and SEC. The report also is available at no charge on the GAO website at http://www.gao.gov.

If you or your staffs have any questions about this report, please contact A. Nicole Clowers at (202) 512-8678 or clowersa@gao.gov. Contact points for our Offices of Congressional Relations and Public Affairs may be found on the last page of this report. GAO staff who made major contributions to this report are listed in appendix VI.

A. Nicole Clowers
Director
Financial Markets and Community Investment

Appendix I: Objectives, Scope, and Methodology

This report examines (1) what is known about the Securities and Exchange Commission's (SEC) organizational culture and (2) SEC's personnel management challenges and its efforts to address these challenges. We focused the scope of our review on all five divisions and one office primarily responsible for implementing the agency's mission—Divisions of Corporation Finance; Enforcement; Investment Management; Economic and Risk Analysis; Trading and Markets; and the Office of Compliance Inspections and Examinations (OCIE). For purposes of this report, we refer to these divisions and office as divisions. In the six divisions, we focused on employees in four occupational categories (accountants, attorneys, examiners, and financial analysts) that account for the majority of SEC employees and on all senior officers in those divisions. We reviewed management consultant reports, and SEC reports, SEC IG reports, and testimonies to describe what is known about SEC personnel management challenges and any agency initiatives (either planned or under way) to address them during the past few years. We reviewed the methodology of the management consultant reports and SEC IG studies and determined that they were sufficiently reliable for the purposes of our report; however, the results should not necessarily be considered as definitive, given the potential methodological or data limitations contained in the studies individually or collectively. We also assessed SEC policies, procedures, and practices against applicable federal regulations related to personnel management, the Office of Personnel Management's (OPM) Human Capital Assessment and Accountability Framework (HCAAF), GAO reports on human capital practices and standards for internal control, and SEC's strategic plan for fiscal years 2010-2015.[1]

---

[1]Human Resources Management in Agencies, HCAAF and HCAAF Systems, Standards, and Metrics, 73 Fed. Reg. 23012, 23027 (Apr. 28, 2008) (codified at 5 C.F.R. § 250.202 (2012)); GAO, *Organizational Transformation: Implementing Chief Operating Officer/Chief Management Officer Positions in Federal Agencies*, GAO-08-34 (Washington, D.C.: Nov. 1, 2007); *Human Capital: Key Principles for Effective Workforce Planning*, GAO-04-39 (Washington, D.C.: Dec. 11, 2003); *Results-Oriented Cultures: Modern Performance Management Systems Are Needed to Effectively Support Pay for Performance*, GAO-03-612T (Washington, D.C.: Apr. 1, 2003); *Human Capital: DOD Needs to Improve Implementation of and Address Employee Concerns about its National Security Personnel System*, GAO-08-773 (Washington, D.C.: Sept. 10, 2008); *Results-Oriented Government: Practices That Can Help Enhance and Sustain Collaboration among Federal Agencies*, GAO-06-15 (Washington, D.C.: Oct. 21, 2005); *Managing Key Results: Key Considerations for Implementing Interagency Collaborative Mechanisms*, GAO-12-1022 (Washington, D.C.: Sept. 27, 2012); and *Standards for Internal Control in the Federal Government*, AIMD-00-21.3.1 (Washington, D.C.: Nov. 1, 1999).

To conduct our work, we examined SEC policies and procedures for
carrying out personnel management responsibilities, including recruitment
and training, performance appraisal, supervision, promotion processes,
and communication within and among SEC divisions. In addition, we met
with SEC's Office of Human Resources and senior leaders from the
divisions to discuss and collect information on their views on SEC's
organizational culture, personnel management challenges, and future
plans to address these challenges. We also interviewed SEC's Inspector
General officials, four former SEC employees, SEC union leaders and
members, two management consultants who previously worked with
SEC, representatives from two industry trade groups, and two academics
with knowledge of SEC personnel management issues to obtain their
views on the agency's organizational culture, personnel management
challenges, and what, if anything, SEC can do to address these
challenges.

We also conducted eight semistructured group interviews with
nonsupervisory staff. Each group interview consisted of employees from
one division to facilitate rapport among the participants. To select
participants to take part in the first six sessions, we relied on the
assistance of SEC union leaders to recruit volunteers from each of the
divisions, To select participants for the last two sessions, we sent e-mails
to nonsupervisory staff who were not union members to invite them to
take part in group interview sessions for employees in the Division of
Enforcement and OCIE, two of the largest divisions at SEC. For each 2-
hour interview, we asked participants to share their views on SEC's
organizational culture, what was working well or not well in relation to
SEC personnel management, and what could be done to address any
challenges.[2] The information we gathered during these interviews
provided an initial understanding of participants' views on these issues
and was used to inform the design of later data collection methods.

Our methods for gathering perspectives from current SEC employees on
organizational culture and personnel management issues included
semistructured one-on-one interviews, focus groups, and two web-based
surveys of all SEC employees (including senior officers) in the selected
divisions and occupational groups. This combination of data collection

---

[2]The results of the in-depth interviews may not be generalized to all SEC employees
because they represent only the experiences of those taking part in the interviews.

techniques was carried out sequentially, so that knowledge gained from one technique could be used to inform the design of the next. For example, based on information learned through our interview efforts, we designed questions used in the focus group effort that followed.[3]

Individual interviews. We interviewed 129 employees (92 nonsupervisory staff and 37 supervisors and senior officers) at SEC headquarters (in person) and regional offices (by telephone or e-mail) during 3 weeks from July through September 2012. We created opportunities for all SEC employees from the six divisions and four occupational categories to meet or communicate with us individually. At headquarters, we established office hours during which employees could speak with GAO analysts. To encourage open communication, we had separate office hours for nonsupervisory and supervisory employees. During the same period, we set up a GAO toll-free phone number and e-mail account to communicate with employees in the regional offices or headquarters who could not attend the office hours. We asked certain key questions of every person and interjected additional questions as appropriate. We also presented SEC Section 962 of the Dodd-Frank Wall Street Reform and Consumer Protection Act (Dodd-Frank Act), which describes the elements of our study.[4] We then asked them to describe

---

[3]For the purpose of our report, we categorized nonsupervisory and supervisory staff by placement under SEC's pay plan. Nonsupervisory staff were in pay grades SK 12-16 for the Division of Enforcement, and SK 12, 13, 14, and 16 for the remaining divisions. Supervisory staff were in pay grade SK 17 for the Division of Enforcement, and SK 15 and 17 for the other divisions. Senior officers were in pay grades SO1-3. These categories were current as of July 2012.

[4]Pub. L. No. 111-203, § 962, 124 Stat. 1376, 1908-09 (2010). Section 962 of the Dodd-Frank Act mandated GAO to evaluate: (A) the effectiveness of supervisors in using the skills, talents, and motivation of the employees of the Commission to achieve the goals of the Commission; (B) the criteria for promoting employees of the Commission to supervisory positions; (C) the fairness of the application of the promotion criteria to the decisions of the Commission; (D) the competence of the professional staff of the Commission; (E) the efficiency of communication between the units of the Commission regarding the work of the Commission (including communication between divisions and between subunits of a division) and the efforts by the Commission to promote such communication; (F) the turnover within subunits of the Commission, including the consideration of supervisors whose subordinates have an unusually high rate of turnover; (G) whether there are excessive numbers of low-level, mid-level, or senior-level managers; (H) any initiatives of the Commission that increase the competence of the staff of the Commission; and (I) the actions taken by the Commission regarding employees of the Commission who have failed to perform their duties and circumstances under which the Commission has issued to employees a notice of termination. § 962(b)(1)(A)-(I).

SEC's organizational culture, what was working well or not in relation to personnel management at SEC, and what could be done to address challenges. Employees were encouraged to talk openly and freely. To maintain the confidentiality of individual responses, we collected and analyzed the information by division and rank only, and aggregated our findings so that no individual comments could be identified.

We conducted a content analysis to summarize key themes that emerged from the individual interviews. Two GAO analysts independently read notes from 23 interviews and made a judgment about appropriate codes that described the themes. The analysts compared their decisions and reconciled any disagreements, resulting in the following set of coding categories: (1) personnel management areas in which SEC has been doing well; (2) areas in which there might be challenges, including views on SEC's organizational culture; (3) any comments on initiatives under way to address the challenges; and (4) any recommendations for addressing the initiatives. This process was replicated several times before finalizing the coding structure. Once the coding structure was finalized, the content of 129 sets of notes was coded by one analyst and then separately reviewed by a second analyst who indicated agreement or disagreement with the code. The two analysts then made changes based on their resolution to those differences.

Focus Groups. We conducted 22 focus groups with approximately 200 randomly selected SEC staff and supervisors at headquarters and in four regional offices (Forth Worth, Texas; Los Angeles, California; Miami, Florida; and New York, New York) from September through December 2012.[5] We selected the regional offices based on factors including (1) the size and significance of the regional office's enforcement and examination activities as well as the significance of the industry that the regional office oversees; (2) efforts made by regional offices to identify and address personnel management issues; and (3) geographical variation. For the focus groups, we randomly selected supervisory and nonsupervisory staff from Enforcement, Corporation Finance, and OCIE from a list SEC provided. Although participants were randomly selected and represented a broad cross-section of employees, our results are not statistically

---

[5]We invited and confirmed 8 to 10 staff for each focus group, but did not record attendance or names in order to ensure confidentiality.

generalizable.[6] We held separate sessions for nonsupervisory and
supervisory staff. [7] For all 22 focus groups, all but a few selected
employees were able to attend.

The moderator used a GAO-developed discussion guide to facilitate each
focus group session and encouraged participants to share their thoughts
and experiences related to SEC personnel management, organizational
culture, and what worked well (or not) in relation to these issues.
Participants also were encouraged to comment on initiatives to address
personnel management challenges and offer suggestions for
improvement. For each of the 22 focus groups, GAO analysts observed
and took notes of the discussion and reviewed them to identify recurring
themes such as training, leadership, performance management,
communication, and organizational culture. One GAO analyst conducted
an initial review of the notes and tabulated the frequency of statements
expressing certain themes, while a second analyst verified the information
to ensure the tabulation was accurate and that the analyst concurred with
the results.

Surveys. From January through March 2013, we conducted two separate
self-administered web-based surveys of all 2,439 listed employees
(nonsupervisors and supervisors) in four occupational categories and six
divisions, and all 86 senior officers in six divisions.[8] That is, we performed
one survey of supervisory and nonsupervisory staff and one of senior
officers. We chose to survey all staff in the targeted divisions and
occupational groups instead of a sample to provide the largest feasible
number of SEC employees a chance to voice their opinions. Each survey
included questions on (1) personnel management issues related to

---

[6]Methodologically, focus groups are not designed to demonstrate the extent of a problem
or to generalize results to a larger population. Instead, they are intended to generate in-
depth information about the reasons for the participants' attitudes on specific topics and
offer insights into their concerns about or support for an issue.

[7]Of the 22 sessions, 11 consisted of only nonsupervisory staff and 11 of only supervisory
staff. Within both these groups, we held single sessions in each of the five locations with
staff from Enforcement and OCIE, which operate both in headquarters and the regional
offices. We held one supervisory and one nonsupervisory session with staff from
Corporation Finance at headquarters.

[8]Our survey population consisted of employees who were employed at SEC as of
September 30, 2012. From this list, we selected all nonsupervisors and supervisors in the
six divisions who were mission-critical employees—accountants, attorneys, examiners,
and financial analysts—and the senior officers in those divisions.

recruitment, training, staff development, and resources; (2)
communication between and within divisions and offices; (3) leadership
and management; (4) performance management and promotions; and (5)
organizational culture and climate. The separate survey of all SEC senior
officers (those at the SO-1, SO-2, and SO-3 pay grades) covered the
same topic areas, but omitted many questions not relevant for senior
officers and included additional questions specifically relevant for senior
officers.

A total of 1,905 nonsupervisors and supervisors responded to our staff
survey for a response rate of 78 percent. A total of 64 senior officers
responded to our senior officer survey for a response rate of 74 percent.
For the staff survey, we carried out a statistical nonresponse bias analysis
using available administrative data and determined that we could not
assume the nonrespondents were missing at random. For this reason, the
results of the staff survey are presented as tabulations from a census
survey. We do not make any attempt to extrapolate the findings to the 22
percent of eligible staff who chose not to complete our survey.

To minimize other types of errors, commonly referred to as nonsampling
errors, and enhance data quality, we employed recognized survey design
practices in the development of the questionnaires and the collection,
processing, and analysis of the survey data. To develop our survey
questions, we drew on information from the one-on-one interviews, focus
group sessions, and prior GAO SEC personnel management surveys. We
pretested the questionnaire with SEC employees. During survey
development, we reviewed the survey to ensure the ordering of survey
sections was appropriate and that questions in each section were clearly
stated and easily comprehended. A GAO survey expert reviewed and
provided feedback on our survey instrument. To reduce nonresponse,
another source of nonsampling error, we undertook an intensive follow-up
effort that included multiple e-mail reminders to encourage SEC
employees to complete the questionnaire. We minimized processing
errors by having a second independent data analyst conduct an accuracy
check of the computer programs used for data analysis. Also, having the
respondents complete questionnaires online eliminated errors associated
with manual data entry. On the basis of our application of these practices
and follow-up procedures, we determined that the data were of sufficient
quality for our purposes.

To analyze the information we obtained from the open-ended survey
responses, we reviewed all the comments and then reviewed the content
of three survey items in more detail to categorize the information into

different themes. For comments related to communication and culture at
SEC, one GAO analyst initially coded all the information and a second
analyst reviewed it separately. Both analysts resolved any coding
discrepancies before finalizing the results. Because of the large number
of comments relating to performance management, we limited our
analysis to the first 150 responses and identified examples of recurring
themes. We coded the comments as described above. Where coding by
the two analysts matched, we selected some responses to provide
anecdotes about perceived issues related to SEC performance
management. The responses are not representative of the views of all
SEC employees. We also reviewed OPM's 2012 Federal Employee
Viewpoint Survey results to obtain additional perspectives from SEC staff
on the agency's personnel management-related issues.[9]

We conducted this performance audit from March 2012 to July 2013 in
accordance with generally accepted government auditing standards.
Those standards require that we plan and perform the audit to obtain
sufficient, appropriate evidence to provide a reasonable basis for our
findings and conclusions based on our audit objectives. We believe that
the evidence obtained provides a reasonable basis for our findings and
conclusions based on our audit objectives.

---

[9]OPM's Federal Employee Viewpoint Survey is a tool that measures employees'
perceptions of whether, and to what extent, conditions characterizing successful
organizations are present in their agencies. Survey results provide valuable insight into
the challenges agency leaders face in ensuring the government has an effective civilian
workforce and how well they are responding. The 2012 Federal Employee Viewpoint
Survey included employees from 82 agencies (constituting 97 percent of executive branch
agencies).

Appendix II: GAO Survey on SEC Personnel and Human Capital Management

From January through March 2013, we conducted two separate, self-administered, web-based surveys of: (1) all 2,439 listed employees (nonsupervisors and supervisors) in four occupational categories and six divisions and (2) all 86 senior officers in six divisions.[1] We chose to survey all staff in the targeted divisions and occupational groups instead of a sample to provide the largest feasible number of SEC employees a chance to voice their opinions. Each survey included questions on (1) personnel management issues related to recruitment, training, staff development, and resources; (2) communication between and within divisions and offices; (3) leadership and management; (4) performance management and promotions; and (5) organizational culture and climate. The separate survey of all SEC senior officers (those at the SO-1, SO-2, and SO-3 pay grades) covered the same topic areas, but omitted many questions not relevant for senior officers and included additional questions specifically relevant for senior officers. The survey is reproduced below.

Survey Introduction

The U.S. Government Accountability Office, an independent agency of Congress, has been mandated by the Dodd-Frank Act (Section 962) to study personnel management at the Securities and Exchange Commission (SEC), including issues related to human capital programs, workforce planning, performance management, and communication. As a part of our study, we are sending this questionnaire to attorneys, accountants, examiners, and financial economists in the Divisions of Corporation Finance, Enforcement, Investment Management, Trading and Markets, Risk Strategy and Financial Innovation, and the Office of Compliance Inspections and Examinations (OCIE) to obtain their opinions about various aspects of working at the SEC.[2] Your cooperation is critical to providing the Congress with complete and balanced information on

---

[1] Our survey population consisted of employees who were employed at SEC as of the end of fiscal year 2012. From this list, we selected all nonsupervisors and supervisors in the six divisions who were mission-critical employees—accountants, attorneys, examiners, and financial analysts—and the senior officers in those divisions. The six divisions were Corporation Finance, Enforcement, Investment Management, Trading and Markets, Economics and Risk Analysis, and the Office of Compliance Inspections and Examinations (OCIE).

[2] The Division of Risk, Strategy, and Financial Innovation changed its name to the Division of Economic and Risk Analysis in June 2013, after our survey was conducted. We will present the survey results consistent with how the information was presented to survey respondents.

how personnel management is functioning across these offices and divisions within the SEC. This questionnaire should take about 30 minutes to complete.

The results of this questionnaire will be used to compile descriptive information on SEC's personnel management. GAO pledges to maintain the confidentiality of the responses to this survey. Your information will be kept confidential and will not be released outside GAO, unless compelled by law or requested by the Congress. Our report will provide results in summary form; individual answers may be discussed, but we will not include any information that could be used to identify individual respondents, and any link between the identification number assigned to your questionnaire and your identifying information will be destroyed.

All of the questions in this survey can be answered by clicking on radio buttons or providing comments in spaces provided at the end of each section. Please complete the questionnaire within 10 business days of receipt. This questionnaire is divided by topic into six sections:

1. Recruitment, Training, Staff Development, and Resources

2. Communication between and within SEC Divisions and Offices

3. Leadership and Management

4. Performance Management and Promotions

5. Organizational Culture and Climate

6. Demographics and Background Information; and

7. Final Comments.

Although your participation is voluntary, we urge you to complete this questionnaire. We cannot develop meaningful information without your frank and honest answers.

Thank you very much for your time.

Survey Results of Nonsupervisors and Supervisors

Note: For each question, the two rows of results correspond to nonsupervisory in the first row and supervisor in the second row.

1. To what extent do you agree or disagree with the following statements on recruitment, hiring and retention? *(Select one response per item.)*

	Strongly Agree/ Somewhat Agree	Neither Agree nor Disagree	Strongly Disagree/ Somewhat disagree	Do Not Know	Not Checked
a. My division/office is able to attract talented and qualified employees.	86.4%	6.4%	5.5%	1.5%	0.2%
	92.6	3.3	3.6	0.3	0.3
b. My division/office retains its most talented and qualified employees.	52.9	16.7	26.9	3.1	0.5
	69.5	12.3	17.4	0.3	0.5
c. Management usually hires employees who are a good fit for SEC's mission.	70.2	14.1	13.1	2.0	0.7
	82.3	8.7	8.5	0	0.5
d. When new people start in jobs in my division/office, they are given enough guidance and training.	38.4	16.1	38.8	5.8	1.0
	65.1	15.4	18.0	1.0	0.5
e. Hiring is sometimes based more on personal connections than on substantive experience or qualifications.	23.5	20.0	41.9	14.0	0.6
	15.4	8.2	73.1	3.1	0.3
f. Overall, SEC's Office of Human Resources provides timely support to my division/office.	14.5	20.0	34.8	29.8	0.8
	21.0	19.5	49.2	9.7	0.5
g. SEC's Office of Human Resources has the necessary expertise to assist in recruiting and hiring qualified employees.	10.6	18.4	31.9	38.5	0.6
	12.8	21.5	46.7	18.0	1.0

2. To what extent do you agree or disagree with the following statements on training and development opportunities? *(Select one response per item.)*

	Strongly Agree/ Somewhat Agree	Neither Agree nor Disagree	Strongly Disagree/ Somewhat disagree	Do Not Know	Not Checked
a. SEC management is committed to the ongoing training and development of staff.	67.0	13.1	18.7	0.8	0.5
	85.1	6.9	6.9	0	1.0
b. SEC needs to invest more in the development of new staff.	72.2	17.9	5.5	3.6	0.8
	62.8	18.5	16.2	0.8	1.8
c. The training I have received over the past three years has provided me skills and experience to meet SEC's needs.	60.3	17.2	20.0	1.9	0.7
	70.3	19.0	9.2	0.3	1.3
d. Employees in my division/office are currently given the same opportunities to participate in training programs and events.	66.8	9.8	16.3	6.3	0.9
	86.2	4.9	6.9	1.3	0.8
e. Management in my division/office needs to do more to address skills gaps.	53.7	26.3	13.5	5.8	0.8
	47.2	27.2	24.4	0.3	1.0
f. Over the past three years, SEC's leadership training has been effective in improving the management skills of supervisors and managers in my division/office.	17.8	22.4	39.7	19.6	0.6
	54.6	19.0	22.6	2.8	1.0

3. For those training opportunities that you have been involved with over the past three years, to what extent, if at all, have the following types of training provided information and knowledge that is directly relevant to your work? *(Select one response per item.)*

	To a great extent	To a moderate extent	To a small extent	To no extent	No basis to judge	Do not know	Not checked
a. Training provided by the SEC University	16.6	38.5	26.8	5.8	8.4	3.0	0.8
	20.0	43.1	26.7	3.9	4.6	1.5	0.3
b. Internal training delivered by SEC staff, but not through SEC University	24.3	41.6	20.0	6.2	5.2	1.8	1.0
	35.1	38.7	20.3	2.0	2.3	1.3	0.3
c. External training or conferences	15.7	28.9	21.2	10.1	19.0	4.1	1.0
	16.9	35.1	18.0	10	16.9	1.3	1.8
d. Computer-based training delivered by Internet	8.2	29.9	31.0	12.8	12.3	4.2	1.6
	6.4	32.8	35.9	9.5	12.6	2.1	0.8

4. Have there been opportunities over the past three years for you to participate in training that provided the latest industry specific knowledge relevant to your job with outside instructors who are experts in the field?

Yes	73.2	80.3
No	18.8	14.4
Do not know	7.1	4.9
Not checked	0.9	0.5

5. In general, how adequate, is the number of training opportunities that provide the latest industry specific knowledge relevant to your job with outside instructors who are experts in the field?

More than adequate	10.9	18.0
Adequate	40.5	42.1
Less than adequate	41.0	35.1
Do not know	7.1	4.6
Not checked	0.6	0.3

6. Over the past 3 years, how many times have you taken part in training that provided the latest industry specific knowledge relevant to your job that included outside instructors who are experts in the field?

Never	11.4	11.3
Once or twice	45.7	38.7
Three or more times	37.8	44.9
Do not know	4.5	4.9
Not checked	0.8	0.3

7. If there are any other issues, details, or information concerning recruitment, training, staff development and resources that you would like us to know about, please use the space below to provide this information.

We will not present detailed comments.

8. To what extent do you agree or disagree with the following statements regarding communication within your division/office and between your division/office and other SEC offices and divisions? *(Select one response per item.)*

	Strongly Agree/ Somewhat Agree	Neither Agree nor Disagree	Strongly Disagree/ Somewhat disagree	Do Not Know	Not Checked
a. Supervisors and managers ensure that employees are included in the flow of relevant information.	47.7	11.6	39.0	1.3	0.3
	73.1	8.0	19.0	0	0
b. My division/office supports open, two-way communication between staff and management.	49.5	13.5	35.4	0.9	0.6
	72.8	10.0	17.2	0	0
c. Information is adequately shared across groups in my division/office.	34.1	14.1	47.5	3.0	1.3
	55.1	14.1	29.0	0.5	1.3
d. Communication across groups in my division/office has improved over the past three years.	33.0	23.3	30.3	12.8	0.7
	64.4	16.9	17.2	1.0	0.5
e. Overall, information and knowledge are shared openly at all levels within my division/office.	29.9	17.0	48.7	3.8	0.7
	52.6	14.6	30.3	1.3	1.3
f. In my division/office, communication between other offices and divisions (such as between OCIE and CorpFin) on work related matters is encouraged.	54.3	18.7	21.5	4.9	0.7
	75.1	14.6	8.7	1.3	0.3

9. In the past 12 months, how often, if at all, did you typically contact employees in the following Home Office divisions or offices for work-related issues such as to coordinate activities or ask for expert advice? *(Select one response per item. Select "Not Applicable" if you work in that division or office.)*

	Daily	One or more times a week	One or more times a month	One or more times in the past 12 months	Never	Do not know	Not applicable	Not checked
a. OCIE	2.5	4.2	11.6	34.3	39.1	1.2	5.8	1.4
	5.4	8.7	27.7	32.1	19.7	0.3	5.4	0.8
b. Division of Enforcement	8.0	5.8	16.6	32.6	21.3	0.8	13.1	1.9
	10	11.0	26.7	32.8	10	0.3	8.5	0.8
c. Division of Corporation Finance	6.0	2.4	9.7	34.7	33.4	1.0	10.9	1.9
	7.4	2.1	17.7	31.0	28.2	0.5	11.0	2.0
d. Division of Investment Management	1.6	1.8	8.8	33.7	45.3	1.2	6.4	1.2
	2.6	4.6	18.7	44.9	23.3	0.5	4.6	0.8
e. Division of Trading and Markets	3.6	2.8	8.8	35.3	40.0	1.2	6.8	1.6
	3.6	6.2	20.3	36.4	26.7	0.8	4.9	1.3
f. Division of Risk, Strategy, and Financial Innovation	0.8	3.0	10.3	23.7	53.4	1.6	5.5	1.6
	1.0	3.9	12.6	38.7	38.2	2.1	3.3	0.3

10. In the past 12 months, how often did employees in the following Home Office divisions or offices get back to you promptly in response to requests for assistance with work-related issues such as to coordinate activities or provide expert advice? *(Select one response per item. Select "Not Applicable" if you work in that division or office or if you did not communicate with that division or office in the past 12 months.)*

	Always or almost always	Most of the time	About half of the time	Some of the time	Never or almost never	Do not know	Not applicable	Not checked
a. OCIE	28.3	17.3	1.4	2.7	2.2	3.0	44.1	1.0
	41.5	25.9	2.3	1.8	0.8	0.8	25.1	1.8
b. Division of Enforcement	32.0	21.3	2.4	3.6	2.1	2.3	35.1	1.4
	39.7	31.3	2.6	3.6	0.5	0.8	21.0	0.5
c. Division of Corporation Finance	28.04	17.4	1.3	3.3	1.9	2.6	43.9	1.6
	29.5	22.1	2.8	2.3	1.0	1.5	40.0	0.8
d. Division of Investment Management	22.9	15.4	1.6	2.9	2.1	3.4	49.9	1.7
	32.6	23.3	6.4	2.8	1.3	2.6	29.5	1.5
e. Division of Trading and Markets	25.4	16.7	1.3	3.1	2.4	3.8	45.3	2.0
	26.7	27.2	4.6	5.1	1.8	2.8	30.8	1.0
Division of Risk, Strategy, and Financial Innovation	22.0	11.1	1.3	1.4	1.6	4.4	55.3	3.0
	26.9	21.3	2.1	1.3	0.8	4.1	42.3	1.3

11. In which location do you currently work?

Home office (Washington, D.C.)	48.6	46.7
A regional or district office	50.8	52.8
Not checked	0.6	0.5

11a. In the past 12 months, how often, if at all, did you typically communicate with employees in the other division or office within your Regional Office for work-related issues such as to coordinate activities or ask for expert advice? *(Select one response per item. Select "Not Applicable" if you work in that Office or Division in your Regional Office.)*

	Daily	One or more times a week	One or more times a month	One or more times in the past 12 months	Never	Do Not Know	Not Applicable	Not Checked
OCIE	9.5	9.9	19.5	28.0	12.1	1.1	17.5	2.4
Division of Enforcement	14.3	8.7	13.4	26.7	8.9	1.1	23.8	3.0

11b. In the past 12 months, how often did employees in the other division within your Regional Office get back to you promptly in response to requests for assistance with work-related issues such as to coordinate activities or provide expert advice? *(Select one response per item. Select "Not Applicable" if you work in that Office or Division or if you did not communicate with that division or office in the past 12 months.)*

	Always or almost always	Most of the time	About half of the time	Some of the time	Never or almost never	Do Not Know	Not Applicable	Not Checked
OCIE	46.1	16.3	1.4	2.3	1.2	1.6	28.9	2.2
Division of Enforcement	39.8	18.7	1.7	2.8	1.0	1.5	30.6	3.9

12. If there are any other issues, details, or information concerning communication between and within divisions and offices that you would like us to know about, please use the space below to provide this information.

We will not present detailed comments.

13. To what extent do you agree or disagree with the following statements
regarding the quality of management and leadership in your
division/office. *(Select one response per item.)*

	Strongly Agree/ Somewhat Agree	Neither Agree nor Disagree	Strongly Disagree/ Somewhat disagree	Do Not Know	Not Checked
a. Supervisors and managers in my division/office are held accountable for achieving results that help SEC meet its goals and priorities.	42.5	13.4	25.0	18.9	0.3
	74.9	6.2	15.1	3.6	0.3
b. In my division/office, the roles and responsbilities of supervisors and managers are clearly defined.	45.7	14.2	32.2	7.7	0.3
	69.2	8.5	21.8	0.3	0.3
c. Supervisors and managers in my division/office are genuinely interested in the opinions of their staff.	54.9	12.2	30.3	1.6	0.9
	73.3	8.7	17.2	0	0.8
d. 360 degree feedback is an effective way for employees to provide feedback on the performance of their supervisors.	50.2	12.0	14.8	22.5	0.5
	47.2	15.9	20.0	16.7	0.3
e. Promotion to management is mostly based on technical skills.	18.1	16.0	47.4	18.5	0
	47.2	17.2	31.3	4.1	0.3
f. Promotion to management is mostly based on the ability to manage people effectively.	13.8	12.5	57.5	15.9	0.4
	41.5	15.9	38.0	4.1	0.5
g. Promotion to management is mostly based on connections that staff have with management.	54.9	14.6	12.4	17.6	0.6
	35.6	19.2	39.5	4.9	0.8
h. There is not much incentive to get promoted into a management position because the salary increase is minimal.	51.6	16.8	20.3	10.9	0.3
	74.1	6.7	17.2	1.3	0.8
i. Over the past 3 years, I have seen SEC staff leave due to being dissatisfied with a supervisor or manager.	57.7	10.0	13.0	18.9	0.4
	46.4	13.3	28.5	10.5	1.3

14. Over the past three years, to what extent, if at all, have the Senior Officers (SOs) in your division/office worked to make improvements in the areas listed below? *(Select one response per item. Please note that "division/office" refers to your division or office (such as Corporation Finance in the Home Office or a Division or Enforcement in a regional office))*

	To no extent	To a small extent	To a moderate extent	To a great extent	No basis to judge	Do not know	Not checked
a. Workforce morale	30.1	27.7	18.6	10.4	7.2	5.7	0.3
	19.7	31.0	27.7	17.7	2.6	1.3	0
b. Collaboration between divisions and offices	16.8	21.7	23.5	14.5	12.2	10.7	0.6
	10.8	19.2	32.6	29.5	4.4	3.3	0.3
c. Staff training focused on specific competencies	14.2	26.1	28.8	13.5	8.3	8.4	0.6
	10.0	23.6	37.2	22.6	3.3	3.1	0.3
d. Transparency in the promotion process	51.6	12.4	5.5	1.9	15.3	12.9	0.4
	34.4	18.7	18.0	8.7	11.5	8.5	0.3

15. Over the past three years, to what extent, if at all, has management solicited employees' ideas and suggestions in developing initiatives designed to improve communication, the performance management system, and training opportunities? *(Select one response per item.)*

Management solicited employees' idea and suggestions in developing...

	To a great extent	To a moderate extent	To a small extent	To no extent	Not aware of any such initiative	Do not know	Not checked
a. Initiatives designed to improve communication	9.1	21.3	20.9	20.3	19.0	8.8	0.6
	20.5	31.5	22.6	11.5	8.5	5.1	0.3
b. Initiatives designed to improve the performance management system	5.0	13.7	17.3	32.8	16.8	13.8	0.6
	7.7	16.9	25.6	20.5	0.8	20.5	8.0
c. Initiatives designed to improve training opportunities	13.5	28.9	23.5	12.2	11.7	9.1	1.1
	28.2	36.9	20.5	7.2	2.8	2.8	1.5

16. Over the past three years, how satisfied have you been with initiatives management developed to improve communication, the performance management system, and training opportunities? *(Select one response per item.)*

	Very satisfied	Somewhat satisfied	Somewhat dissatisfied	Very dissatisfied	Not aware of any such initiative	Do not know	Not checked
a. Initiatives designed to improve communication	6.6	27.2	16.4	16.6	23.2	9.0	1.1
	13.9	44.9	17.2	9.7	10.0	4.1	0.3
b. Initiatives designed to improve the performance management system	2.3	17.1	18.1	30.2	19.0	11.6	1.8
	9.2	29.0	21.5	27.4	7.7	3.9	1.3
c. Initiatives designed to improve training opportunities	14.1	37.9	15.1	10.3	12.4	8.5	1.7
	25.1	48.2	12.6	5.6	4.6	2.8	1.0

17. Are the numbers of supervisors and managers currently in your division/offices more than is needed, less than is needed, or an appropriate amount given the current workload?

More than needed	24.6	14.1
An appropriate amount	50.3	51.8
Less than needed	15.1	32.6
Do not know	9.2	1.3
Not checked	0.8	0.3

18. Are the numbers of levels of supervisions currently in your division/offices more than is needed, less than is needed, or an appropriate amount given the current workload?

More than needed	26.2	13.9
An appropriate amount	58.6	69.2
Less than needed	7.4	14.6
Do not know	7.1	1.8
Not checked	0.8	0.5

19. What is your current, direct supervisor's position or title?

Branch Chief	20.0	2.3
Exam Manager	7.0	2.6
Assistant Director	56.0	39.5
Associate Director	6.0	44.6
Other	10.4	10.8
Not checked	0.6	0.3

20. To what extent do you agree or disagree with the following statements regarding your current direct supervisors? *(Select one response per item.)*

	Strongly Agree/ Somewhat Agree	Neither Agree nor Disagree	Strongly Disagree/ Somewhat disagree	Do Not Know	Not Checked
a. Is knowledgeable in the issue areas I conduct my work.	83.9	4.2	9.9	1.0	1.0
	88.2	1.5	9.2	0.5	0.5
b. Has the skills and expertise to be an effective supervisor or manager.	72.1	7.5	18.4	1.2	0.8
	79.2	4.1	14.9	0.5	1.3
c. Does a good job in sharing information.	69.6	9.0	19.4	0.9	1.0
	78.0	7.4	13.3	0.5	0.8
d. Clearly defines goals and expectations.	66.6	10.2	21.6	0.6	1.0
	73.3	9.2	15.9	0.5	1.0
e. Provides useful and constructive feedback.	65.3	11.9	20.1	1.0	1.6
	70.5	9.5	16.7	1.0	2.3
f. Will listen to me if we have differing ideas or approaches.	76.8	7.0	13.4	1.8	1.0
	86.1	2.8	8.5	1.3	1.3
g. Is willing to change his or her position when there is compelling information.	73.5	8.3	12.6	4.3	1.4
	82.1	6.2	8.0	2.8	1.0
h. Gives me the flexibility I need to do my job effectively.	83.2	6.3	8.3	0.7	1.5
	88.7	4.1	5.6	0.5	1.0
i. Spends too much time closely monitoring my work.	10.3	14.4	73.0	1.1	1.2
	10.8	12.1	75.1	1.0	1.0

21. If there are any other issues, details, or information concerning leadership and management at SEC that you would like us to know about, please use the space below to provide this information.

We will not present detailed comments.

22. To what extent do you agree or disagree with the following statements regarding how SEC management recognizes and rewards performance in your division/office? *(Select one response per item.)*

	Strongly Agree/ Somewhat Agree	Neither Agree nor Disagree	Strongly Disagree/ Somewhat disagree	Do Not Know	Not Checked
a. Overall, senior officers deal effectively with poor performing supervisors and managers.	5.3	9.9	56.2	28.4	0.1
	24.9	15.1	46.7	13.3	0
b. Overall, supervisors and managers deal effectively with poor performing staff.	9.6	12.4	51.1	26.6	0.3
	28.5	12.8	55.1	3.1	0.5
c. Supervisors and managers are quick to provide feedback to staff whose performance is unacceptable.	9.5	12.2	33.8	43.5	1.0
	36.9	21.0	35.9	5.9	0.3
d. I know what is expected of me regarding my work performance.	74.5	10.3	14.2	0.8	0.3
	86.4	4.6	8.5	0.5	0
e. My direct supervisor provides sufficient performance feedback.	67.9	12.3	17.4	1.8	0.7
	74.9	9.0	14.6	1.0	0.5
f. The criteria for rewarding staff are clearly defined.	17.5	14.0	63.8	4.5	0.3
	39.5	16.7	42.6	0.8	0.5
g. The criteria for promoting staff are clearly defined.	10.0	13.6	68.9	7.3	0.3
	37.7	18.5	41.3	1.8	0.8
h. For promotion opportunities, the quantity of reviews, exams, or cases is more important than their complexity or difficulty.	19.7	19.0	23.2	37.4	0.8
	11.5	17.4	61.0	9.5	0.5
i. The opportunities in my division/office to get promoted into a management position are limited.	78.7	8.3	7.1	5.5	0.5
	83.1	7.2	9.5	0.3	0
j. Favoritism is typically not an issue in promotions.	15.5	15.5	46.2	22.2	0.6
	54.4	11.8	29.7	3.9	0.3

	Strongly Agree/ Somewhat Agree	Neither Agree nor Disagree	Strongly Disagree/ Somewhat disagree	Do Not Know	Not Checked
k. Promotions go to those who most deserve it.	19.7	16.4	44.5	18.5	1.0
	57.7	16.7	21.5	3.1	1.0
l. There is a clear link between my performance and recognition of it.	37.6	17.4	38.6	5.5	1.0
	60.5	14.1	24.6	0	0.8
m. Current performance incentives are effective tools to motivate employees to perform well.	12..0	14.2	67.2	5.9	0.7
	14.9	15.4	68.5	0.8	0.5

23. To what extent do you agree or disagree with the following statements regarding SEC's current performance management system? *(Select one response per item.)*

	Strongly Agree/ Somewhat Agree	Neither Agree nor Disagree	Strongly Disagree/ Somewhat disagree	Do Not Know	Not Checked
a. SEC's 5-point rating system allows for an accurate representation of my performance over the rating period.	25.6	15.7	52.4	5.8	0.6
	45.4	11.8	41.3	1.3	0.3
b. How competencies are weighted accurately reflects the relative importance of my work.	19.1	19.3	50.4	10.3	0.9
	30.5	17.2	49.7	2.1	0.5
c. SEC's performance management system uses relevant criteria to evaluate my performance.	31.1	18.0	44.0	5.5	1.4
	46.7	12.8	39.2	0.5	0.8
d. SEC's performance management system allows supervisors and managers to have a meaningful discussion with their staff on how they are performing.	32.6	17.7	43.3	5.1	1.2
	52.6	15.1	30.5	0.5	1.3
e. SEC's performance management system provides consistent standards for rewarding performance.	16.4	16.3	57.9	8.6	0.9
	36.4	16.2	44.6	2.6	0.3
f. Changes need to be made to increase transparency in the process used to rate my performance.	60.1	19.2	13.3	6.1	1.3
	44.6	26.2	26.9	1.0	1.3

	Strongly Agree/ Somewhat Agree	Neither Agree nor Disagree	Strongly Disagree/ Somewhat disagree	Do Not Know	Not Checked
g. Calibration of performance ratings by management improves fairness in the performance management system.	20.2	20.0	36.5	22.1	1.3
	50.3	13.1	33.1	3.3	0.3
h. Employee performance appraisals are fair and appropriate under SEC's performance management system.	20.1	21.0	42.8	14.8	1.2
	51.8	18.5	26.9	1.5	1.3

24. if there are any other issues, details, or information concerning performance management and promotions at SEC that you would like us to know about, please use the space below to provide this information.

We will not present detailed comments.

25. To what extent do you agree or disagree with the following statements regarding different aspects of organizational culture and climate within your division/office? *(Select one response per item.)*

	Strongly Agree/ Somewhat Agree	Neither Agree nor Disagree	Strongly Disagree/ Somewhat disagree	Do Not Know	Not Checked
a. There is an atmosphere of trust in my division/office.	45.1	13.4	40.0	1.1	0.4
	59.0	10.5	30.3	0.3	0
b. Employee morale is generally high most of the time.	29.8	14.5	54.1	1.2	0.4
	38.2	18.2	42.6	0.8	0.3
c. I have a voice in decisions that affect me and my work environment.	38.3	17.9	41.8	1.3	0.8
	63.1	12.1	23.6	0	1.3
d. Management in my division/office has taken steps to improve employee morale.	30.2	18.5	44.7	6.2	0.4
	52.6	16.4	30.3	0.5	0.3
e. Supervisors and managers in my division/office tolerate honest mistakes as learning experiences.	56.4	15.5	19.2	8.2	0.7
	75.1	11.3	12.3	1.0	0.3

	Strongly Agree/ Somewhat Agree	Neither Agree nor Disagree	Strongly Disagree/ Somewhat disagree	Do Not Know	Not Checked
f. Protecting investors is sometimes hampered by staff or managers who view firms as places they can potentially work at in the future.	10.2	7.0	71.5	10.9	0.4
	5.9	4.9	86.4	2.1	0.8
g. There are clearly defined policies and procedures for doing my work.	56.8	17.9	24.1	0.9	0.3
	73.3	12.6	13.3	0.3	0.5
h. Innovative ideas are encouraged in my division/office.	50.1	17.5	30.1	1.4	0.9
	67.4	13.9	17.7	0	1.0
i. Fear of public scandals has made SEC overly cautious and risk-averse.	54.5	16.7	21.0	7.5	0.3
	57.4	14.6	24.6	2.3	1.0
j. In my view, the fear of being wrong makes supervisors and managers in my division/office reluctant to take a stand on important issues.	49.3	15.1	29.5	5.8	0.3
	41.5	12.8	44.4	0.8	0.5
k. In my view, the fear of being wrong makes senior officers in my division/office reluctant to take a stand on important issues.	46.7	15.1	26.6	10.9	0.8
	44.1	13.6	38.5	3.6	0.3

26. If there are any other issues, details, or information concerning the organizational culture or climate at the SEC or in your division/office that you would like us to know about, please use the space below to provide this information.

We will not present detailed comments.

Survey Results of Senior Officers

1. To what extent do you agree or disagree with the following statements on recruitment, hiring and retention? *(Select one response per item.)*

	Strongly Agree/ Somewhat Agree	Neither Agree nor Disagree	Strongly Disagree/ Somewhat disagree	Do Not Know	Not Checked
a. My division/office is able to attract talented and qualified employees.	92.2	1.6	6.3	0	0
b. My division/office retains its most talented and qualified employees.	84.4	6.3	9.4	0	0
c. When new people start in jobs in my division/office, they are given enough guidance and training.	71.9	10.9	12.5	1.6	3.1
d. Hiring is sometimes based more on personal connections than on substantive experience or qualifications.	3.1	3.1	92.2	0	1.6
e. Overall, SEC's Office of Human Resources provides timely support to my division/office.	14.1	17.2	64.1	3.1	1.6
f. SEC's Office of Human Resources has the necessary expertise to assist in recruiting and hiring qualified employees.	6.3	15.6	71.9	6.3	0

2. To what extent do you agree or disagree with the following statements on training and development opportunities? *(Select one response per item.)*

	Strongly Agree/ Somewhat Agree	Neither Agree nor Disagree	Strongly Disagree/ Somewhat disagree	Do Not Know	Not Checked
a. SEC needs to invest more in the development of new staff.	68.8	23.4	6.3	1.6	0
b. The training I have received over the past three years has provided me skills and experience to meet SEC's needs.	65.6	26.6	7.8	0	0
c. Management in my division/office needs to do more to address skills gaps.	51.6	21.9	21.9	1.6	3.1
d. Over the past three years, SEC's leadership training has been effective in improving the management skills of supervisors and managers in my division/office.	70.3	15.6	4.7	9.4	0

3. For those training opportunities that you have been involved with over the past three years, to what extent, if at all, have the following types of training provided information and knowledge that is directly relevant to your work? *(Select one response per item.)*

	To a great extent	To a moderate extent	To a small extent	To no extent	No basis to judge	Do not know	Not checked
Training provided by the SEC University	15.6	43.8	28.1	6.3	6.3	0	0
Internal training delivered by SEC staff, but not through SEC University	26.6	57.8	9.4	1.6	3.1	0	1.6
External training or conferences	12.5	43.8	28.1	1.6	12.5	0	1.6
Computer-based training delivered by Internet	4.7	29.7	50.0	9.4	4.7	0	1.6

4. If there are any other issues, details, or information concerning recruitment, training, staff development and resources that you would like us to know about, please use the space below to provide this information.

We will not present detailed comments.

5. To what extent do you agree or disagree with the following statements regarding communication within your division/office and between your division/office and other SEC offices and divisions? *(Select one response per item.)*

	Strongly Agree/ Somewhat Agree	Neither Agree nor Disagree	Strongly Disagree/ Somewhat disagree	Do Not Know	Not Checked
a. My division/office supports open, two-way communication between staff and management.	93.8	4.7	1.6	0	0
b. Information is adequately shared across groups in my division/office.	81.3	9.4	7.8	0	1.6
c. Communication across groups in my division/office has improved over the past three years.	82.8	9.4	7.8	0	0
d. Overall, information and knowledge are shared openly at all levels within my division/office.	67.2	15.6	17.2	0	0
e. In my division/office, communication between other offices and divisions (such as between OCIE and CorpFin) on work related matters is encouraged.	93.8	3.1	3.1	0	0

7. To what extent do you agree or disagree with the following statements regarding the quality of management and leadership in your division/office. *(Select one response per item.)*

	Strongly Agree/ Somewhat Agree	Neither Agree nor Disagree	Strongly Disagree/ Somewhat disagree	Do Not Know	Not Checked
a. In my division/office, the roles and responsbilities of senior officers are clearly defined.	82.8	3.1	14.1	0	0
b. In my division/office, the roles and responsbilities of non-senior officer supervisors and managers are clearly defined.	90.6	3.1	4.7	0	1.6
c. Senior officers in my division/office are genuinely interested in the opinions of their employees.	95.3	3.1	1.6	0	0
d. Non-senior officer supervisors and managers in my division/office are genuinely interested in the opinions of their staff.	95.3	1.6	1.6	0	1.6
e. 360 degree feedback is an effective way for employees to provide feedback on the performance of their supervisors.	54.7	17.2	20.3	0	7.8
f. Promotion to management is mostly based on technical skills.	56.3	28.1	15.6	0	0
g. Promotion to management is mostly based on the ability to manage people effectively.	62.5	21.9	15.6	0	0
h. There is not much incentive to get promoted into a management position because the salary increase is minimal.	42.2	10.9	42.2	3.1	1.6
i. Over the past 3 years, I have seen SEC staff leave due to being dissatisfied with a supervisor or manager.	29.7	12.5	37.5	20.3	0

8. Are the numbers of supervisors and managers currently in your division/office more than is needed, less than is needed, or an appropriate amount given the current workload?

More than needed	7.8
An appropriate amount	51.6
Less than needed	35.9
Do not know	3.1
Not checked	1.6

9. Are the numbers of levels of supervisions currently in your division/office more than is needed, less than is needed, or an appropriate amount given the current workload?

More than needed	4.7
An appropriate amount	70.3
Less than needed	20.3
Do not know	3.1
Not checked	1.6

10. If there are any other issues, details, or information concerning leadership and management at SEC that you would like us to know about, please use the space below to provide this information.

We will not present detailed comments.

11. To what extent do you agree or disagree with the following statements regarding how SEC management recognizes and rewards performance in your division/office? *(Select one response per item.)*

	Strongly Agree/ Somewhat Agree	Neither Agree or Disagree	Strongly Disagree/ Somewhat disagree	Do Not Know	Not Checked
a. Overall, senior officers deal effectively with poor performing supervisors and managers.	56.3	17.2	23.4	3.1	0
b. I know what is expected of me regarding my work performance.	79.7	7.8	12.5	0	0
c. My direct manager provides sufficient performance feedback.	60.9	18.8	15.6	4.7	0
d. The opportunities in my division/office to get promoted into a management position are limited.	68.8	4.7	25	1.6	0
e. There is a clear link between my performance and recognition of it.	59.4	20.3	18.8	0	1.6
f. Current performance incentives are effective tools to motivate employees to perform well.	18.8	18.8	59.4	1.6	1.6

12. To what extent do you agree or disagree with the following statements regarding SEC's current performance management system? *(Select one response per item.)*

	Strongly Agree/ Somewhat Agree	Neither Agree or Disagree	Strongly Disagree/ Somewhat disagree	Do Not Know	Not Checked
a. SEC's 5-point rating system allows for an accurate representation of my performance over the rating period.	50.0	7.8	31.3	10.9	0
b. How competencies are weighted accurately reflects the relative importance of my work.	32.8	20.3	34.4	9.4	3.1
c. How competencies are weighted accurately reflects the relative importance of my employees' work.	31.3	15.6	46.9	4.7	1.6
d. SEC's performance management system uses relevant criteria to evaluate my performance.	51.6	12.5	28.1	6.3	1.6
e. SEC's performance management system allows supervisors and managers to have a meaningful discussion with their staff on how they are performing.	62.5	9.4	26.6	1.6	0
f. The time it takes me to develop, review, and formalize performance assessments under SEC's current performance management system is unreasonable.	79.7	4.7	12.5	3.1	0
g. SEC's performance management system provides consistent standards for rewarding performance.	43.8	25	29.7	1.6	0
h. Changes need to be made to increase transparency in the process used to rate my performance.	26.6	34.4	23.4	14.1	1.6
i. Cal bration of performance ratings by management improves fairness in the performance management system.	71.9	9.4	17.2	1.6	0
j. Employee performance appraisals are fair and appropriate under SEC's performance management system.	70.3	17.2	10.9	0	1.6

13. If there are any other issues, details, or information concerning performance management and promotions at SEC that you would like us to know about, please use the space below to provide this information.

We will not present detailed comments.

14. To what extent do you agree or disagree with the following statements regarding different aspects of organizational culture and climate within your division/office? *(Select one response per item.)*

	Strongly Agree/ Somewhat Agree	Neither Agree or Disagree	Strongly Disagree/ Somewhat disagree	Do Not Know	Not Checked
a. There is an atmosphere of trust in my division/office.	73.4	7.8	17.2	1.6	0
b. Employee morale is generally high most of the time.	54.7	20.3	25	0	0
c. I have a voice in decisions that affect me and my work environment.	92.2	4.7	1.6	0	1.6
d. Senior officers in my division/office tolerate honest mistakes as learning experiences.	90.6	7.8	0	0	1.6
e. Protecting investors is sometimes hampered by staff or managers who view firms as places they can potentially work at in the future.	0	3.1	96.9	0	0
f. There are clearly defined policies and procedures for doing my work.	81.3	12.5	6.3	0	0
g. Innovative ideas are encouraged in my division/office.	92.2	4.7	3.1	0	0
h. Fear of public scandals has made SEC overly cautious and risk-averse.	62.5	12.5	25	0	0
i. In my view, the fear of being wrong makes supervisors and managers in my division/office reluctant to take a stand on important issues.	21.9	12.5	62.5	3.1	0
j. In my view, the fear of being wrong makes non-senior officers and managers in my division/office reluctant to take a stand on important issues.	29.7	17.2	53.1	0	0

15. If there are any other issues, details, or information concerning the organizational culture or climate at the SEC that you would like us to know about, please use the space below to provide this information.

We will not present detailed comments.

Appendix III: Ratio of Staff to Supervisors and Senior Officers, Fiscal Years 2008-2012

Section 962 of the Dodd-Frank Act requires us to review whether there is "excessive number of low-level, mid-level, or senior-level managers." We did not find standards for evaluating "excessive" number of supervisors have not been established. Table 16 illustrates the ratio of supervisors to nonsupervisors. Table 17 illustrates the ratio of senior officers to nonsupervisors, and table 18 illustrates the ratio of senior officers to supervisors.

Table 16: Ratio of Supervisors to Nonsupervisors (per every 100 nonsupervisory staff), Fiscal Years 2008-2012

Division	Supervisors to nonsupervisors				
	FY08	FY09	FY10	FY11	FY12
Division of Corporation Finance	24.1	23.2	21.0	26.8	23.4
Division of Investment Management	31.3	31.6	29.7	18.8	32.0
Division of Economic and Risk Analysis	a	a	29.6	28.1	16.7
Division of Trading and Markets	23.6	23.0	23.9	24.4	18.8
Division of Enforcement	28.3	27.3	22.7	10.9	16.2
Office of Compliance Inspections and Examinations	33.4	33.1	30.2	28.4	35.3

Source: GAO analysis of SEC data.

[a]There are no data for Division of Economics and Risk Analysis in 2008 and 2009 because the division was created in September 2009.

Table 17: Ratio of Senior Officers to Nonsupervisors (per every 100 nonsupervisory staff), Fiscal Years 2008-2012

Division	Senior officers to nonsupervisors				
	FY08	FY09	FY10	FY11	FY12
Division of Corporation Finance	3.3	3.1	2.6	6.5	3.7
Division of Investment Management	6.3	6.1	5.9	3.1	6.0
Division of Economic and Risk Analysis	a	a	3.7	0	2.1
Division of Trading and Markets	7.5	6.2	6.7	4.1	6.1
Division of Enforcement	3.6	3.4	3.8	4.2	3.4
Office of Compliance Inspections and Examinations	3.1	3.0	2.9	6.1	3.8

Source: GAO analysis of SEC data.

[a]There are no data for Division of Economics and Risk Analysis in 2008 and 2009 because the division was created in September 2009.

Table 18: Ratio of Senior Officers to Supervisors (per Every 100 Supervisory Staff), Fiscal Years 2008-2012

Division	Senior officers to supervisors				
	FY08	FY09	FY10	FY11	FY12
Division of Corporation Finance	13.5	13.2	12.3	24.3	15.8
Division of Investment Management	20.0	19.4	20.0	16.7	18.8
Division of Economic and Risk Analysis	a	a	12.5	0	12.5
Division of Trading and Markets	32.0	26.9	28.1	16.7	32.3
Division of Enforcement	12.6	12.3	16.9	38.1	21.2
Office of Compliance Inspections and Examinations	9.4	9.1	9.5	21.3	10.7

Source: GAO analysis of SEC data.

[a]There are no data for Division of Economics and Risk Analysis in 2008 and 2009 because the division was created in September 2009.

Appendix IV: Percentage of Staff Who Left SEC, Fiscal Years 2008-2012

Among its provisions, Section 962 of the Dodd-Frank Wall Street Reform and Consumer Protection Act requires us to review turnover rates within SEC subunits.[1] While staff turnover rates could be used to identify potential areas for improvement and further develop current supervisors, officials from the Merit Systems Protection Board noted that turnover was not a good indicator of poor supervision for several reasons. For example, staff may leave to pursue opportunities with a different employer or a different career path, or for personal reasons. SEC officials also indicated that staff facing potential removal or termination often would resign or retire, rather than going through removal or termination. Tables 19 and 20 show the percentage of staff who left SEC from fiscal years 2008 through 2012 from headquarters and the 11 regional offices, respectively. Table 21 shows the total number of staff who left SEC during the same period.

Table 19: Headquarters Staff Who Left SEC, Fiscal Years 2008-2012

		FY08		FY09		FY10		FY11		FY12	
Reason for separation	Employee category	Percentage separated	Total staff	Percentage separated	Total staff	Percentage separated	Total staff	Percentage separated	Total staff	Percentage separated	Total staff
Retirement	Nonsupervisors	0.8%	900	0.2%	937	1.2%	1,008	1.8%	914	0.6%	1027
	Supervisors	1.5%	196	0.0%	199	2.2%	224	2.7%	183	1.3%	234
	Senior officers	0.0%	41	0.0%	40	8.7%	46	11.1%	45	2.0%	51
Resignation	Nonsupervisors	4.4%	900	1.8%	937	2.1%	1,008	2.7%	914	4.0%	1027
	Supervisors	3.1%	196	1.5%	199	1.3%	224	3.8%	183	2.1%	234
	Senior officers	4.9%	41	12.5%	40	19.6%	46	8.9%	45	5.9%	51
Removal or termination	Nonsupervisors	0.4%	900	0.6%	937	1.0%	1,008	0.9%	914	0.7%	1027
	Supervisors	0.0%	196	0.5%	199	0.0%	224	1.1%	183	0.9%	234
	Senior officers	0.0%	41	0.0%	40	0.0%	46	2.2%	45	3.9%	51

Source: GAO analysis of SEC data.

[1]Pub. L. No. 111-203, § 962(b)(1)(F), 124 Stat. 1376, 1909 (2010).

Table 20: Staff Who Left SEC from 11 Regional Offices, Fiscal Years 2008-2012

Reason for separation		FY08		FY09		FY10		FY11		FY12	
		Percentage separated	Total staff	Percentage separated	Total staff	Percentage separated	Total staff	Percentage separated	Total staff	Percentage separated	Total staff
Retirement	Nonsupervisors	0.8%	927	0.4%	954	1.1%	981	1.2%	861	1.0%	987
	Supervisors	3.7%	191	1.5%	197	5.0%	221	1.8%	168	1.7%	237
	Senior officers	4.2%	24	0.0%	23	8.0%	25	4.8%	42	3.7%	27
Resignation	Nonsupervisors	3.2%	927	1.2%	954	1.5%	981	2.8%	861	3.4%	987
	Supervisors	1.6%	191	2.0%	197	0.9%	221	4.2%	168	1.7%	237
	Senior officers	0.0%	24	8.7%	23	0.0%	25	2.4%	42	3.7%	27
Removal or termination	Nonsupervisors	0.5%	927	0.1%	954	0.3%	981	0.1%	861	0.8%	987
	Supervisors	0.0%	191	0.0%	197	0.0%	221	0.6%	168	0.4%	237
	Senior officers	0.0%	24	0.0%	23	4.0%	25	0.0%	42	0.0%	27

Source: GAO analysis of SEC data.

Table 21: All Staff Who Left SEC, Fiscal Years 2008-2012

Reason for separation		FY08 Percentage separated	Total staff	FY09 Percentage separated	Total staff	FY10 Percentage separated	Total staff	FY11 Percentage separated	Total staff	FY12 Percentage separated	Total staff
Retirement	Nonsupervisors	0.8%	1,827	0.3%	1,891	1.2%	1,989	1.5%	1,775	0.8%	2014
	Supervisors	2.6%	387	0.8%	396	3.6%	445	2.3%	351	1.5%	471
	Senior officers	1.5%	65	0.0%	63	8.5%	71	8.0%	87	2.6%	78
Resignation	Nonsupervisors	3.8%	1,827	1.5%	1,891	1.8%	1,989	2.8%	1,775	3.7%	2014
	Supervisors	2.3%	387	1.8%	396	1.1%	445	4.0%	351	1.9%	471
	Senior officers	3.1%	65	11.1%	63	12.7%	71	5.7%	87	5.1%	78
Removal or termination	Nonsupervisors	0.5%	1,827	0.4%	1,891	0.7%	1,989	0.5%	1,775	0.7%	2014
	Supervisors	0.0%	387	0.3%	396	0.0%	445	0.9%	351	0.6%	471
	Senior officers	0.0%	65	0.0%	63	1.4%	71	1.1%	87	2.6%	78

Source: GAO analysis of SEC data.

Appendix V: Comments from the Securities and Exchange Commission

UNITED STATES
SECURITIES AND EXCHANGE COMMISSION
WASHINGTON, D.C. 20549

THE CHAIR

July 3, 2013

A. Nicole Clowers
Director
Financial Markets and Community Investment
U.S. Government Accountability Office
441 G Street, NW
Washington, DC 20548

Dear Ms. Clowers:

Thank you for the opportunity to respond to the draft report, *"Securities and Exchange Commission: Improving Personnel Management Is Critical for Agency's Effectiveness (GAO-13-621)."* We believe that the Government Accountability Office's (GAO) study of the Securities and Exchange Commission's personnel management practices and organizational culture contains useful recommendations to help strengthen personnel management at the SEC. We agree with the seven recommendations and will continue our efforts to address them.

We are pleased that the GAO acknowledges the steps the SEC has taken to address its organizational culture and personnel management challenges. The agency's staff and leaders remain committed to building upon and sustaining an organizational culture where innovation, collaboration, and transparency are encouraged. In addition, we believe our efforts in enhancing our personnel management programs have yielded significant results. We recognize that we still have work to do in these areas and are committed to ensuring that progress continues.

As mentioned in the report, the SEC has taken steps toward identifying and addressing its workforce competency gaps. The most recent progress in this area includes the establishment of a workforce and succession planning function, which is staffed by three subject matter experts within the Office of Human Resources (OHR). This team's primary responsibility is to provide tools, systems, and reports for analyzing the agency's workforce supply and demand to determine gaps and risks. In addition, the team will coordinate all workforce succession planning inquiries and activities across the agency and develop and disseminate succession planning strategies. OHR anticipates fully operationalizing this function in FY14.

The report also acknowledges the SEC's progress in the implementation of its performance management system. We agree that the system reflects the characteristics of an effective system. The system has been fully validated and the competencies used in the system were the result of an SEC-wide study that included all employees. As a result, we successfully implemented pay for performance for non-bargaining unit employees during this past rating cycle and were able to establish a clear link between pay and performance. We are in the

Ms. A Nicole Clowers
Page 2

process of assessing the impact of the new system on non-bargaining unit employees and expect favorable outcomes.

We acknowledge that improvements can be made with the performance management system. By fully implementing the performance management system, offering additional training opportunities to managers, and offering information sessions to employees, we will effectively manage the agency's full transition into the new system. As the report mentions, the SEC currently is engaged with the National Treasury Employees Union (NTEU) on the appraisal process for bargaining unit employees. We are confident that we will soon reach agreement with NTEU on this issue. This will allow the agency to experience the full and positive impact of the system's design.

Meeting the challenges related to improving intra-agency communication is a top priority for the SEC, and we have taken meaningful steps toward overcoming these longstanding barriers. In addition to the positive examples included in the report, we also highlight the following:

- The Office of Compliance, Inspections and Examinations' (OCIE) Office of Chief Counsel (OCC) serves as a liaison between examination staff and the SEC's divisions. The OCC regularly communicates with the divisions of Enforcement, Trading and Markets (TM), Investment Management (IM), and Corporation Finance (CF), as well as the Office of International Affairs (OIA), on various issues, often making contact with the divisions on behalf of examiners or vice versa. For example, the Aberrational Performance Inquiry – an initiative to combat hedge fund fraud by identifying abnormal investment performance – involved significant collaboration between Enforcement, OCIE, OIA, and the Division of Economic and Risk Analysis (DERA);

- Every division and several offices have dedicated enforcement liaisons who communicate with Enforcement staff on a regular basis regarding ongoing investigations and enforcement recommendations. In addition, TM has a designated OCIE liaison. Recently, OCIE's OCC hired two staff members whose duties include being a liaison to TM and IM;

- OCIE has formed nine specialized working groups in an effort to focus on key industry risk areas in the financial markets. Over 600 staff participate in the specialized working groups from all regional offices and the SEC's home office, including staff from IM, TM, the Office of the Chief Accountant, the Office of Credit Ratings, the Office of Investor Education and Advocacy, CF, DERA, and several areas within Enforcement, including its Office of Market Intelligence, Asset Management Unit, Structured and New Products Unit, and Market Abuse Unit. Through such broad participation, these working groups facilitate the sharing of information on key risk areas and industry trends across many divisions and offices of the SEC.

- The SEC establishes cross-divisional working groups for the economic analysis of each rule being written.

Ms. A Nicole Clowers
Page 3

- The SEC created the Internal College of Supervisors, a monthly meeting with staff across the agency who deal in any way with supervision of large broker-dealers. Organized by TM, staff from most divisions attend and report on relevant activities over the last month.

- The Office of the Chief Operating Officer and the Offices of the Managing Executives for the divisions and offices regularly communicate and coordinate on initiatives impacting the agency as a whole, including topics such as technology, leasing, budgeting, and the Tips, Complaints and Referrals program. Enforcement and OCIE also have added a shared Regional Operations Liaison to assist in communicating and coordinating with the 11 regional offices on SEC initiatives and business operations. Finally, the SEC has added an Assistant Regional Director of Operations in each regional office to improve communication and consistency across the agency as a whole.

As the report states, "both SEC staff and external stakeholders have started to see positive effects from the recent efforts to bolster communication and collaboration." We appreciate this acknowledgement and will continue to leverage these results in our continuous improvement efforts.

In addition, OHR has prioritized the development of an HR Accountability System and Plan. The most recent progress in this area includes directing an SEC staff member with subject matter expertise to begin work on this effort. OHR has developed key milestones and deliverables in anticipation of full implementation by the end of this calendar year. Once implemented, the system will specifically address the concerns cited in the report regarding the alignment of human capital practices to SEC strategic goals.

Thank you for the consideration that you and your staff have shown our agency. We remain committed to investing time and resources to improve the organizational culture and personnel management at the SEC. We are very confident that the efforts underway, once fully implemented, will further strengthen the areas cited in the report while continuing to provide results in the identified areas of success.

If you have any questions or would like to further discuss this response, please contact Lacey Dingman, Director, Office of Human Resources, at (202) 551-7500.

Sincerely,

Mary Jo White
Chair

Appendix VI: GAO Contact and Staff Acknowledgments

GAO Contact	A. Nicole Clowers, (202) 512-8678 or clowersa@gao.gov

Staff Acknowledgments	In addition to the contact above, Triana McNeil (Assistant Director), Carl Barden, Bethany Benitez, Pamela Davidson, Simin Ho, Chir-Jen Huang, Catherine Hurley, Stuart Kaufman, Jonathan Kucskar, Tarek Mahmassani, Marc Molino, and Barbara Roesmann made key contributions to this report.

GAO's Mission	The Government Accountability Office, the audit, evaluation, and investigative arm of Congress, exists to support Congress in meeting its constitutional responsibilities and to help improve the performance and accountability of the federal government for the American people. GAO examines the use of public funds; evaluates federal programs and policies; and provides analyses, recommendations, and other assistance to help Congress make informed oversight, policy, and funding decisions. GAO's commitment to good government is reflected in its core values of accountability, integrity, and reliability.
Obtaining Copies of GAO Reports and Testimony	The fastest and easiest way to obtain copies of GAO documents at no cost is through GAO's website (http://www.gao.gov). Each weekday afternoon, GAO posts on its website newly released reports, testimony, and correspondence. To have GAO e-mail you a list of newly posted products, go to http://www.gao.gov and select "E-mail Updates."
Order by Phone	The price of each GAO publication reflects GAO's actual cost of production and distribution and depends on the number of pages in the publication and whether the publication is printed in color or black and white. Pricing and ordering information is posted on GAO's website, http://www.gao.gov/ordering.htm. Place orders by calling (202) 512-6000, toll free (866) 801-7077, or TDD (202) 512-2537. Orders may be paid for using American Express, Discover Card, MasterCard, Visa, check, or money order. Call for additional information.
Connect with GAO	Connect with GAO on Facebook, Flickr, Twitter, and YouTube. Subscribe to our RSS Feeds or E-mail Updates. Listen to our Podcasts. Visit GAO on the web at www.gao.gov.
To Report Fraud, Waste, and Abuse in Federal Programs	Contact: Website: http://www.gao.gov/fraudnet/fraudnet.htm E-mail: fraudnet@gao.gov Automated answering system: (800) 424-5454 or (202) 512-7470
Congressional Relations	Katherine Siggerud, Managing Director, siggerudk@gao.gov, (202) 512-4400, U.S. Government Accountability Office, 441 G Street NW, Room 7125, Washington, DC 20548
Public Affairs	Chuck Young, Managing Director, youngc1@gao.gov, (202) 512-4800 U.S. Government Accountability Office, 441 G Street NW, Room 7149 Washington, DC 20548